Are you seriously considering starting up a home business? Before you embark on this new adventure, let Sharon Carr dispel some common myths:

MYTH: I'll never be able to get together the substantial capital needed for starting a home business.

TRUTH: "... most big businesses started out in a bedroom, garage or kitchen. You don't need a lot of money to begin. But you do need imagination and a passion for your chosen business."

* * * * * * *

MYTH: A home business means I can work anytime I want—sleep 'til ten and work 'til one in the morning—what freedom!

TRUTH: "Remember all the years you worked a nine-to-five job?...Do exactly the same thing when your office is down the hall."

* * * * * * *

MYTH: I want to do everything myself—be totally self-sufficient, so I won't have the hassle of dealing with other people.

TRUTH: "Being self-sufficient is one thing, but don't get ridiculous... hire the best people you can get and pay them a competitive salary." "Seek network support... get active in organizations and support groups...networking = leads!"

HOME BUSINESS 101 is your ticket to learning the "how-to's" (and the "how not to's") of building a successful, rewarding home career.

Home Business 101

Home Business 101

Sharon Carr

Fleming H. Revell Company
Publishers
Old Tappan, New Jersey

Library of Congress Cataloging-in-Publication Data

Carr, Sharon.
    Home business 101 / Sharon Carr.
        p.   cm.
    ISBN 0-8007-5329-1
    1. Home-based businesses.   2. New business enterprises.
    I. Title.
    HD62.7.C358   1989
    658′.041—dc20
                                                            89-33413
                                                                CIP

Copyright © 1989 by Sharon Carr
Published by the Fleming H. Revell Company
Old Tappan, New Jersey 07675
Printed in the United States of America

Acknowledgments

THIS BOOK is dedicated to my one-in-a-million husband, Bob. He has been my helper and friend throughout this endeavor and is always there giving total support above and beyond the call. Without his assistance on everything from cut-and-paste duties, proofreading, and household help to practically feeding me intravenously through long periods of writing, this book would not have been possible. Thanks for being so special and believing in me!

Unending gratitude goes to my wonderful business coach, Juanell Teague, for her keen insight into current trends which initiated the idea for this book. Had it not been for her, the book would still be in draft form. Special thanks to Linkie Seltzer and Bobbi Moore for their expert advice, editing, and sharing.

Artist David Ortiz took pictures out of my mind and expressed them so well on paper. A big thanks goes to him for his talent, which is found in the cartoons throughout this book.

Finally, I appreciate all the home-based business professionals who contributed to this book by taking part in my research questionnaires and interviews. Thanks for giving your time and input so graciously.

Contents

Introduction

CONGRATULATIONS! You have decided to take the plunge and start your own home-based business! Confucius said, "A journey of ten thousand miles begins with but a single step." To succeed, just keep on stepping. Establishing your home-based office will be scary and wonderful, frustrating and uplifting, isolating and rewarding, draining and stimulating. And, it will be worth every effort. You are fulfilling the American dream of having your own business and being your own boss.

The frustration of trying to find one source to help me set up my own home-based business precipitated this book. When starting out, one needs well-rounded, thorough, and easy-to-understand data. This book is written to bridge the gaps other sources leave. You can count on getting the nuts and bolts you need in this one, unique, self-help book. You have the opportunity to participate in this book through the questionnaires, checklists, exercises, and action plans that are provided. These are all carefully aimed at developing you and your business.

As a Christian, I am concerned that my God-given talents and abilities are used to their fullest extent for God's glory. But I am not alone with such a concern.

As I have spoken to various groups, I have found many people who want to stay at home to be close to their families and at the same time want to use and develop their business abilities.

So while I am aware that many women in particular will be interested in reading this book, the practical principles in it apply to men as well as women, and of course will be of help to non-Christians as well as Christians.

The information covers everything, including basic business helps, managing time and stress, finding motivation, marketing strategies, customer service, business equipment, and more. By the time you finish this book, you will know how to be more effective, more productive, and run an efficient office with the least strain on you, your family, and your business. The majority of these ideas will work for the majority of people.

My "hands-on" experience consists of over six years in my own home-based speaking and consulting business. I have provided consulting assistance for small businesses and large corporations on setting up and maintaining their offices.

Information from home-business owners was obtained through one-on-

one interviews and through questionnaires. Their quotes and ideas are used throughout the book to give other viewpoints. A wide range of businesses gave input, including a reinsurance consultant, a certified public accountant, a secretarial service, artist, image consultant, banker, professional speaker, and many others. The purpose of interviewing other home businesses is for you to gain from their various experiences and perspectives. Their stories are included to tell you not only how they got started but also what works and doesn't work for them. More expertise for the book was gathered from AT&T, State Farm Insurance, IBM, several CPA's, business consultants, and others.

The United States Department of Labor predicts that half of the country's work force could be working at home in ten to fifteen years. Over 8 million Americans are currently operating businesses in their homes, according to the Bureau of Labor Statistics. Futurists including Faith Popcorn are saying this figure will double by the end of the century.

Many corporations are discovering the practicality of having employees set up in-home branch offices to save overhead costs. It makes especially good sense for salespeople to work out of the house rather than take up office space.

I promise that if you follow the steps in this book you will get results! I want to save you from going through the frustrating trials and errors that I did. When I started my business, I wish someone would have made these how-to's available for saving time, energy, and money. Now, let's get started on our journey.

Home Business 101

BEFORE

reading this book

AFTER

reading this book

1
Mental Setup

**IF YOU FAIL TO PLAN,
YOU PLAN TO FAIL**

THE FIRST STEP in starting your own business is to believe in yourself. Set yourself up mentally by expecting the very best of yourself and your home-based business. Remember that most big businesses started out in a bedroom, a garage, or a kitchen. You don't need a lot of money to begin. But you do need imagination and a passion for your chosen business.

One common thread running through all the home-based business success stories is that ordinary people discovered a need and capitalized on it. Many are not millionaires in a monetary sense, but they are very rich in job satisfaction, pride in their work, and quality of life. When other home-business owners were asked what most contributed to their success, 99 percent replied "perseverance and believing in myself." Many people who previously had very successful positions in a corporate atmosphere made the choice to be their own bosses.

$ $ $ Success Briefs $ $ $

Anita Williams, now a free-lance writer, was the president of an advertising agency. She realized that because of the stress of corporate pressures and politics, she was losing her ability to be creative. That was her main reason for starting her home business. She comments, "I found myself and my creativity again by having my own business." After five years of happily running this thriving business, she has expanded by combining her writing skills and marketing skills with those of her husband, who also has his own home business.

Doug Coleman, a sales trainer/consultant, realized his opportunities were limited as long as he continued working for someone else. With the experience and abilities he had developed over the years, he decided to find a need and fill it. He now trains others to sell and present themselves in the marketplace. After only four years in his own business, he is in the process of expanding his training-and-consulting service by starting a school for speakers. "I am making a better living now than I was in my nine-to-five job. My goal is to have an organization that operates on autopilot in two years so I can retire." To make the business work, he has reinvested a portion of his profits.

Previously a supervisor of a computer center, Eileen Heifner started her business to be at home with a partially handicapped child. She began making antique porcelain dolls in her basement as gifts. The demand was so great as her dolls gained exposure that the business grew rapidly. She now sells doll kits to individuals and stores all over the country and even teaches customers how to start their own doll-making business. She employs two part-time people and one full-time secretary to keep up with the incoming orders. A new talent surfaced from writing kit instructions—having booklets on doll-making published. Her business is so popular that she recently received an offer to start her own television series.

$ $ $

Whether these people started a home-based business out of necessity, job satisfaction, or a sense of independence, they all have the true spirit of entrepreneurism. How exciting it is to fulfill your personal and career goals. Anyone can do it once you capture the spirit and want it badly enough. When you are down or discouraged, pick yourself up and start again. With determination and persistence, you can do it!

There are many advantages to having a home business. Some of the main benefits are:

- You can start it in your spare time (evenings, weekends)
- You can stay in your regular job for income while building it
- Flexibility in work hours
- You are home with the family/children
- You can begin with minor capital
- You incur no overhead expenses (office costs, day care)
- You can grow and expand at your own speed
- You are your own boss

Now that you've decided to start your own business, let's take it step by step. You cannot begin with a vague course of action; you must have a game plan. Making a plan in writing leaves less to chance. Being self-employed requires a lot of commitment, hard work, energy, and drive. Determine your level of commitment and define your game plan by filling in your responses to the questions below.

My Game Plan

- I want to be self-employed because: _____
_____ .
- Realistically, I need to make $ _____ a month.
- To discover if my product/service is marketable, I have researched these areas: _____
_____ .
- My main purpose for having my own business is: _____
_____ .
- To develop and market the business, I am willing to do whatever it takes. My commitment will be (specify time and money): _____
_____ .

- I have chosen this field because my education and/or experience will give me credibility (list education, experience, and any hands-on knowledge):

  _____

  _____ .

- My confidence level is (on a scale of 1–10, with 1 being low and 10 being high): 1 2 3 4 5 6 7 8 9 10.
- The "help resources" I can turn to for mental support or ideas are (list names of a possible mentor, former fellow worker, friend, minister, etc.):

  _____

  _____ .

Your answers will give you a good measuring stick of how committed you really are to your business. If you noticed any weak areas while filling in this game plan, concentrate on improving them. Statistics tell us that we each spend at least 2,500 hours a year or 100,000 total hours in our office in our lifetime. To spend this much time in a home business takes mental preparation and true commitment.

Be Passionate About What You Are Doing

The Small Business Administration says the single biggest reason for the failure of new businesses is that "people choose fields in which they have little or no knowledge or experience." Be sure you choose something that reflects your background and expertise. It not only will give you greater credibility when, and if, you apply for a business loan, but it will also increase your chance of achieving your goals.

In short, you will be best at doing the things you love most! You *must* love the line of work you have chosen for your business or you will not feel "driven" to succeed. Passion is an important element to your success. Make a point to keep growing by increasing your knowledge in your specific field. If you love what you are doing, you will be hungry for knowledge and have the burning desire necessary to learn and grow.

A well-known educator and speaker, Brian Tracy, notes, "If you spend one extra hour a day studying or taking notes in your particular field, in five years you will be a NATIONAL AUTHORITY on the subject." But, what is the prerequisite? To love what you are doing enough to even *want* to study an hour a day. The time, energy, and work you will expend to accomplish your goals will require passion.

Various means of study might include watching specific TV programs on your business subject, taping your sales approach for improvement, doing research at the library, or joining a particular organization so you can further your education.

You will be honest and true to yourself when you choose to do your "own thing." Isn't that what life is all about? If you love your field and it reflects your background, you have everything going for you. I like the way James Michener puts it:

Master in the Art of Living

You draw no distinction between your work or your play, your labor or your leisure, your mind or body, your love or religion. You hardly know which is which.

You simply pursue your vision of excellence through whatever you are doing and you leave it to others to decide whether you are working or playing.
Because, to yourself, you are always doing BOTH.

James Michener

FIND THE MOTIVATION TO SUCCEED

Oh! The agony of dragging yourself out of bed in the morning. Somehow, when you are your own boss and working at home you think you have the right to sleep late. Feeling that you "deserve" to watch television on an extended basis or take a nap in the afternoon wears off quickly when you realize you have to hustle to make the business work. Are you having trouble getting motivated? Anyone have a firecracker? How about a crane to help pull you out of bed in the morning?

Are you ready to attack the day? Take note of how you are dressed. You won't get much work done sitting around in your robe. If you are in lounging clothes, you will feel like lounging. *Dress for the job you are doing.* When cleaning the house, you dress in grubbies, right? When washing the car or mowing the lawn, you dress in jeans or cutoffs. If you intend to get any work done in your office, you *must* dress the part. To be successful, you must dress and think success!

Dress like an executive and you will feel like one. (This is not to say you need to dress in a business suit every day.) Be sure you are dressed and prepared for a busy day. Men, be sure you have shaved. Women, be sure you have makeup on and hair combed. Then you won't need to stop in the middle of the day for repairs or a change of clothes.

Use your past job experience to make a difference. Make your home-office environment better than your past experience. When you were working for someone else what things did you like that you could recreate in your own office? What things didn't you like that you could avoid? Check off the *positive* things you would like to recreate. Then add other things to the list too.

Positives	**Negatives**
— Building rapport with others	— Office gossip
— Beginning the day at 8:00 A.M.	— Distractions/Interruptions
— Stopping for lunch on time	— Wasting money
—	—
—	—

A study by a Dallas consulting service says that home workers tend to be independent, self-motivated, and comfortable with being alone. You will be responsible for yourself. There will be no one else to blame when things go wrong, no other department to figure taxes or pay benefits, no one to ask about vacations or time off.

I have a very responsible position here—
If anything goes wrong, I am responsible!

Dealing With the Isolation

Missing the "big office atmosphere" from your last job will be new to you in the beginning; however, as time goes by, you will like the quietness of your own home office. I wasn't at all sure about working at home because I had always worked in large offices with heavy activity around me. It was hard to imagine what a day would be like without people standing in my doorway interrupting with questions or having to solve an immediate problem. But, after a few weeks, it was wonderful! It is natural to miss the camaraderie of people being around and the sounds of office machinery. You'll grow to love your new surroundings. The things you won't miss are: fighting traffic to and from work, packing a lunch, being dumped on when you first walk in, or rushing to a department meeting.

One way to deal with the loneliness is to have a stereo or radio in your office. It makes you feel less alone. Also, make a point of stopping to stretch or make a phone call once in a while. This helps you adjust to not having others around. Go out to lunch with a best friend once a week. Or, meet with a buddy from your past place of employment so you do not lose any friendships. This will help you gain a new perspective about what you are and are not missing. You will start feeling more positive and professional about your home office

When to Stop and Start. Remember all the years you worked a nine-to-five job when you had to get up each morning and out of the house at a certain time to arrive at work precisely on time? Do exactly the same thing when your office is down the hall. It is important to START AND STOP ON TIME! Set the alarm and get up each day with a goal in mind of when to "hit" the office. Set the specific times you are planning to work and stop.

Quitting on time so that you have some social or family life is difficult when you work at home because your work is always there. One home professional told me she closes the office door to psychologically say to herself that work is finished until the next day.

Tip: If you have a hard time calling work to a halt, it helps to use an alarm to help you stop at a reasonable hour.

Keeping hours like this will not give you much structure:

Office Hours

OPEN most days about 9 or 10
Occasionally as early as 7,
but SOME DAYS
as late as 12 or 1.

We CLOSE about 5:30 or 6
Occasionally about 4 or 5
But, sometimes as late as 11 or 12.
SOME DAYS or afternoons we aren't here at all
And, lately, I've been here just about all the time
Except when I'm someplace else,
But I should be here then, too.

Fighting Burnout

How do you motivate yourself when you feel burned-out or discouraged or in a rut? It's easy—change something! Do things differently to give yourself a boost.

- Exercise really helps eliminate burnout. Ride a bike, take a brisk walk, or stop by the gym for a workout.
- Listen to cassette tapes on some topic of interest.
- Read an inspirational article.
- Call a friend who encourages you.

Your enthusiasm is only hiding out, taking a break for a while. To find it again, *saturate your mind* with information on your business. Listen to cassette tapes or read books that have been inspiring to you. Visit your local library and read success stories. Don't let the temporary circumstances make a negative impact. Do something that gives you a change of pace and before you know it you'll be back to your old self again. Think positive!

Set up rewards to motivate yourself. If you get finished with a particular project by noon, you can reward yourself by taking time to read the newspaper. If you work for an hour on that dreaded filing task, allow yourself a fifteen-minute break to sit on the patio with an iced tea. These breaks are a home-based business *bonus!*

Tip: If you plan a reward while you are working, you will have more incentive to do the job and get it done faster.

SEEK NETWORK SUPPORT

There are many benefits to networking. One of the main benefits is that networking = leads! It also supplies you with people who are willing to share, solve problems, and give you emotional support. Networking is the only way to find out what other people are encountering. You can ask questions like "Who do you know that could . . . ?" "Where can I find out . . . ?" "What do you do when . . . ?" People are very willing to share and chances are they will benefit from your knowledge too.

$ $ $ Success Brief $ $ $

When I asked Barbara Brabec, well-known author of home-business books, what things most contributed to her success she said networking was number one. "Even after eight years in business, I continue to develop and expand my network of both 'small business' friends and 'big business' contacts. Through this network I am always able to get inside information when it is needed. But, more importantly, my network is my best marketing tool. By seeking out individuals who express an interest in the work I'm doing, and making it easy for them to pass my name on to others, I have automatically formed a strong word-of-mouth advertising base. As people help me get ahead in business, I also help those individuals in my network whenever an opportunity presents itself."

$ $ $

Go to seminars, conferences, or any informational courses where you can meet people with similar interests. Why is it important to get involved?

1. To reinforce what you are doing correctly
2. To make profitable business contacts
3. To give you motivation
4. To gain insight from others in your field
5. To correct a mistake before you make it

Get active in organizations and support groups. There are many networking clubs that have entrepreneurial members. This kind of support can be very beneficial personally and professionally.

The networking process reminds me of raising a child and feeling you are the only parent going through a particular situation. As soon as you begin talking with other parents, you discover they are experiencing the same situation and you feel support. Making contacts with people who are going through the same frustrations and challenges will give you insight. It is nice to know you are not alone!

How do you find these organizations?

- Call your local chamber of commerce. They will send you a list of clubs and organizations in your area with contact names and phone numbers.
- Go to the library. They have complete listings of organizations.
- Check the local newspaper. They usually list community organizations and meeting times.

Before Joining an Organization

Be sure to take advantage of your visitor status before making a decision to join or not. Most groups allow one to two visits. Only allow yourself to spend time and dues to belong to a group that is beneficial to you and your business. Here are some questions to ask an organization before joining:

- What do they offer their members—newsletters? workshops? conventions? seminars?
- How much networking time is given at meetings?
- What costs are there during the year—dues? meals? special functions? exhibits? directories?
- Is membership due on calendar-year basis or prorated if you join in the middle of the year?
- Is there a membership directory? If you join now will you miss getting into the directory for the entire year? What information is included (name and number only or a blurb about your business)?
- Do they allow you to advertise in the directory—at what cost?
- Are you allowed to purchase membership list labels for advertisement purposes?

Get all the information and weigh what you will *give* to and what you will *get* from each organization. With all the facts, you can then make an informed decision. It is hard for me to believe when I hear some new members saying, "They didn't tell me membership dues are figured on a calendar year and I just paid a full year's dues last month," or, "I didn't know they had all these hidden costs besides the initial fee," or, "The people in this group are so unfriendly and cold."

Your time is valuable. Do not rush into anything; you could be sorry later. If you don't like the people involved in a group, don't join! If you think the contacts or the networking will benefit your type of business, it may be an organization worth serious consideration.

Find a Mentor

One home-based graphics artist commented on how important it is to have a "mentor" you can call on for help. Knowing someone who has an existing business in your field is extremely valuable. Find a mentor you can trust and "pick his brain" when you need ideas or have questions. Most people are happy to share their knowledge and love to take new entrepreneurs under their wings. It is a privilege for a person to be asked to be a mentor. It shows how highly you view his or her advice as a professional.

FROM DREAMING TO ACHIEVING

How do you turn dreams into reality?

An associate pastor said it best when he wrote, "Each year is just a pocketful of days that you empty out like coins on your dresser to see what you finished with." How are you going to spend your pocketful of days?

First of all, be sure your dreams match your abilities or the odds will be against you. Close your eyes and picture yourself and your business where you would like to be one year from now. Then, picture where you want to be five years from now. When you can see what you want, you have your goal. Begin setting small, daily goals. What are goals? They are dreams that haven't come true yet.

> *Successful people are dreamers who have found a dream too*
> *exciting, too important, to remain in the realm of fantasy,*
> *and who, day by day, and hour by hour, toil in the service*
> *of their dream until they can touch it with their hands and*
> *see it with their eyes.*

Take time to develop your *plan of action:* After you set your goals, be sure to write them down and post them where you can see them each day. This will increase your chances of reaching each goal. Set both business *and* personal goals.

SELF-MANAGEMENT PLAN OF ACTION

Self-management skills can be improved by setting goals and taking action. List your goals for the next five days, what action you will take to reach the goal, and what the benefit will be. Number them according to their importance. Each time you accomplish and check off a goal, add another.

Examples:

GOAL: *#3*   I will . . . handle paperwork more efficiently
ACTION: by . . . sorting all papers into categories.
BENEFIT TO ME: Higher productivity.

GOAL: *#2*   I will . . . finish my XYZ project
ACTION: by . . . dividing it into small segments.
BENEFIT TO ME: Controlling overwork and frustration.

GOAL: *#1*   I will . . . stop procrastinating
ACTION: by . . . making a daily To-Do List.
BENEFIT TO ME: Will be more effective and feel more sense of
                             accomplishment

      *   *   *   *   *   *   *   *   *

GOAL: #__   I will . . . _____
ACTION: by . . . _____
BENEFIT TO ME: _____

GOAL: #__   I will . . . _____
ACTION: by . . . _____
BENEFIT TO ME: _____

GOAL: #__   I will . . . _____
ACTION: by . . . _____
BENEFIT TO ME: _____

    I like what Charles Kettering says about the future: "My interest is in the future because I'm going to spend the rest of my life there." Doesn't it make sense then, to *plan* for your future? Did you know you will be in the top percentile of the nation if you set goals? The majority of us do not set any short-term or long-term goals, even though we know it works.

    So, dare to dream and turn the dream into goals. Whether that means dreaming toward financial goals or making your home business more successful, *go for it!* I encourage you to grab and achieve all life has to give. But, to know what you want to grab, you must first dream, set a goal, and then set out to attain it. Then, there is nothing that can stop you. You *can* do it!

USING ENERGY LEVELS FOR PRODUCTIVITY

Energy peaks and valleys strongly influence your quality and quantity of work. Are you sharp and quick in the mornings? Is your mind "on" before your feet hit the floor?

   To find out whether you are a morning or afternoon person, discover when your energy peaks and valleys are each day. If you dig in the moment you enter the office and work at a steady pace until lunch, you are a morning person. If you are a slow starter in the morning but whiz through work later in the day, then you are an afternoon person. Once you are aware of the role energy levels play, you can plan your day around them for higher productivity.

"I *Must* Be a Morning Person."

Energy Peaks. These hours are the best of the day—when we get the most done and feel our very best. Find out when your energy is high and choose this time to begin projects that take the most concentration and attention. Do the hardest, most involved tasks in these energy peak times.

Energy Valleys. It's mid-afternoon and you really accomplished a great deal this morning. But, now it's 2:00 P.M. and the familiar energy slump attacks. This *is not* the time to deal with an irate customer, write an important contract, or plan a brainstorming session. That doesn't mean you do nothing when you are in an energy slump. Match your energy level to the job. Here are some constructive ideas for using this time to your advantage:

- *Make phone calls.* This is an excellent time of the day to return and initiate phone calls.
- *Check tickler files.*
- *Clean top of desk.* Go through your "in basket" and gather up all pieces of paper on your desk. Put the phone messages in one pile.
- *Read.* Catch up on reading your business journals, etc.
- *File.* A small pile takes only a few minutes to clear away, but when a pile grows to three inches, it can take hours. If you have a person who does the filing for you, use the time to note in the upper righthand corner where you would like each paper filed. This not only saves the filing person time, but also saves you from interruptions like, "Where did you want this filed. . . ?"
- *Prepare ahead.* Check your calendar. Make an outline of work for an upcoming deadline.

How Can You Change a Valley Into a Peak? There *is* something you can do to revive your energy. Did you know it is a fact that exercise renews energy? Step outside and breathe deeply as you jump up and down or simply walk around. Exercise increases oxygen which enhances circulation and alertness.

Eating a light lunch will help you feel less sluggish in the afternoons. If you eat a four-course meal, chances are that no matter what your energy level is, you won't be able to keep your eyes open.

Tip: When you hire other people, find out when their peaks and valleys are too. Learning about an employee's highs and lows gives you a gauge to the best and worst times to request the major or minor projects.

THE RIGHT WAY TO TALK TO YOURSELF

Go ahead—talk to yourself! But listen to discover whether your self-talk is negative or positive. How you think will determine how positive or negative your self-talk is. Our minds are the sum total of what we think, believe, and do. That's why you have to believe in yourself.

Have you ever gotten up in the morning and said, "Yuk! It's raining and I know it will be a lousy day." Have you ever remarked to someone, "I get strep throat twice a year," or, "I always have financial problems. I'll never get ahead." How you talk to yourself is crucial to your success or failure. Your self-talk will cause you to fulfill your own prophecy—good or bad. In short, this means chances are 100 percent that you will fulfill your own feelings and thoughts about yourself during the day. Why not? You've even verbalized the doom. If a rainy day spells *B-A-D* day, then it definitely will be disastrous. If you believe you will catch strep twice a year, your body will accommodate your thoughts. If you think you will never get ahead financially, it's for certain that you won't. Be careful of the way you talk to yourself. What you believe the consequence or outcome to be can make it happen.

Program Your Mind for Success! Positive versus negative self-talk is the difference you need to feel great about yourself and things around you. Don't let yourself say or think negative thoughts. When your attitude is right, the world seems right and things run more smoothly. Here are some tips on how to acquire a positive attitude:

1. Say to yourself, "I have the confidence and ability to do what needs to be done today.
2. Make yourself speak positively about everything for an entire day: your problems, your work, your health, your family.
3. Matthew 28:20 says that the Lord is with you always, even to the end of the age. Believe it! Stop trying to handle things by yourself. Live each day knowing that He is with you every step of the way.

Let this positive attitude spill over into everything you do. See things happen the way you *want* them to happen. Have you ever tried positive self-talk when making a sales call? I do it all the time. As I'm picking up the phone I think to myself, *This company needs to hear my self-management program and I know I'll arrange a program date.* It works very well.

Carry this self-talk another step further. Try it when looking for a parking space. As you are pulling into any parking lot, begin visualizing someone pulling out of a close parking space. Your self-talk might go like this, "Okay, I'm here. Someone can pull out now to make room for me." I usually get there to find someone's car backing out at exactly the right moment. Try it!

Visualize yourself succeeding at everything you do in your business or personal life. It is imperative to see yourself being successful. When Chris Evert was asked what makes her a winner, she responded by saying that before a game she visualizes herself returning every ball. She practices the game over and over in her mind and pictures herself winning.

Tomorrow when you wake up, find something *good* about yourself when you look in the mirror. No matter what the circumstances or weather, decide you *will* have a successful day. Self-talk is a powerful tool. Use it—positively!

2
Physical Office Setup

"OOPS!"

AVOID CHOOSING A TEMPORARY LOCATION. That never works out! Don't make the mistake I did when setting up my office at home. I started with a desk and typewriter in a corner of our master bedroom. Getting motivated was difficult, not to mention the lack of space to spread out. Talk about an office that wasn't conducive to work! It was all I could do to keep from plopping myself across the bed and doing nothing the entire day. Just the thought of that comfortable bed made me want to forget all about working. Then, I got smart and converted a rarely used guest bedroom into an office. What a difference!

No matter how practical a physical location may seem, remember, it must be comfortable too. If you have to pick up the table before dinner or take down the TV trays each evening, frustration will set in and sabotage your office. The setting up and tearing down will be too much bother.

HOW TO CHOOSE THE BEST LOCATION

To discover the best location for your home office, narrow down your alternatives by asking yourself these questions:

- Do you prefer being near windows? Be sure outside activities will not be distracting to you.
- Is it better for you to be around family/home sounds or would you prefer complete isolation? How important is your privacy?
- What time of day will you be doing most of your work—morning, afternoon, or evening? Do you need light from windows or lamps?
- Will you enjoy having your office in this particular spot or would you choose it because it is the most "practical" place? For instance, if there is a vacant room in your home that you have always disliked because it is dark or hot, this is *not* a good place to set up.
- Do you need to consider being near a door to have a private entrance for clients?

Of course the ideal situation is a permanent area. One CPA who has his business at home told me, "Having a permanent space for my office was the best idea that worked for me." Psychologically, as well as physically, you *need* to have your own special place. This is what provides the incentive for work and for being at your best.

Determining Factors

If you are lucky enough to have more than one area to choose from, here are some specifics to consider before making a decision:

- Is there enough room for a desk, computer, or any other equipment you may need?
- Are there electrical outlets and a telephone jack?
- Is the area in a path that will cause too much traffic from other family members when going from one place in the house to another?
- Does the space have proper heating and cooling (especially if a closet, garage, or storage area is under consideration)?
- Is there good light?

Some offices were born out of a large walk-in closet. If you have a den or large area, you may be able to split and block it off with a temporary wall or room divider. Of course, using a spare bedroom is the perfect solution! You can really fix it up to feel like an office. Here are some ideas:

- Install shelves across one office wall behind the area where your desk will be.
- A built-in credenza with shelves, drawers, and cabinets all the way across one wall gives the home office a classy look. This will add space, countertop, and a place for books.

Turning the clothes closet into an office storage area works well when you:

- Remove the closet doors and clothes rod, then build shelves from the ceiling to halfway down the wall.
- Place two-drawer file cabinets all the way across the closet opening. It will look like you have built-ins and function extremely well. (*See* illustration on page 30.)

Did you know most office furniture stores have designers who specialize in space management? They usually do not charge for visiting your home to help with ideas. Many times they will give you special prices if you purchase the office furniture from their store. If you simply cannot picture the best location for your desk, files, computer, they can help you as they are trained in these areas.

Lighting

Lighting is important. If you have windows, place your desk so that you face the light. Sitting with the sunlight behind you will always place you in your own shadow. Use lamps to your best advantage by forming a triangle of light around the room. Notice where the electrical plugs are located in the room so you won't need extension cords strewn all over the floor.

Tip: If you are going to have a computer in the office, seriously consider having a ceiling fan, with or without a light, to compensate for the extra heat a computer puts out. Ceiling lights with fans can be installed inexpensively by an electrician whether you have an existing ceiling outlet or if one needs to be added.

YOUR GUIDE TO SELECTING EQUIPMENT

When considering what major-dollar items you will need to start up, take time to shop around to be sure what you get is what you need. Yes, you might "outgrow" some of your equipment and need to update it later.

$ $ $ Success Brief $ $ $

William Howsley, a reinsurance consultant who works out of his home, says, "buying equipment or supplies as the need presents itself rather than purchasing everything in the beginning was critical to my financial success.

Sometimes what you 'think' you need at the start is not what you really need once you get settled in. For this reason, it is a good idea to consider renting some equipment on an 'as needed' basis."

$ $ $

Many computer and copier equipment companies are recognizing the increasing demand for home-sized models. They are designing and producing smaller, more compact equipment. Check into these wonderful inventions to determine whether they will be right for you. Do not purchase anything without comparing prices and features.

Before you are ready to buy equipment, be sure you can afford it. If you go into debt, it will be more difficult to see the light at the end of the financial tunnel. In the beginning you need to see profits and you'll grow to resent the equipment if those profits are tied up with creditors.

$ $ $ **Success Brief** $ $ $

Diana Stein was a technical trainer for a large corporation when she decided to start looking for career alternatives that would give her a flexible schedule to spend more time with her family. She and her partner, Linda Salisbury, started OMNI Training to provide technical and managerial training, consulting, and brokering services. "We feel it is really important to keep our overhead expenses down and save for items we need instead of borrowing money and going into debt." Their policy is to save at least 25 percent of what they make and put it back into the business. "We spend only when we have saved enough to pay cash."

$ $ $

Here is a list of big-dollar purchases you may need for your office. Place a check mark in front of the items you want to research. Then check your budget, shop for prices, compare, and call rental stores before making any final decision.

Major $$ Items

__ **TELEPHONE.** If you don't have a jack, have one installed with an extension phone in your home office. Check into costs of owning your own phone versus renting one from your local phone company. According to AT&T, most home businesses start out with a single-line phone. There are several features to consider that add a minimal fee to your monthly phone bill.

Call Forwarding: You can automatically transfer your incoming calls to another number so your calls can follow you wherever you go. Or you can have your calls sent somewhere else (such as when you go on vacation).

Call Waiting: This feature gives you a second line at less cost. When you are already on the phone, a soft tone at ten-second intervals signals you that someone else is trying to call you. At the same time, the person with whom you are talking will hear a slight "click" on the line while the person calling you will hear the regular ringing signal. *Note:* If a third caller tries to reach you while you have two calls connected, the caller will hear a busy signal.

You can also add a "hold" button, automatic dialer or multi-buttons, conference three-way calls, speaker phone, or a programmable dialer to redial any number you input.

Telephone Book Listing: You can either have an additional phone installed with a new number or add an extension phone. If the telephone company knows you are using it as a business phone they will try to insist that you buy a business listing. The advantages of subscribing to a business line are:

1. Your business name and phone number will be listed in both the White Pages and Yellow Pages.
2. You will be in control of after-hours calls either by not answering or by taking the calls on an answering machine.

For a business listing, you will be charged approximately two and a half times more than a private line. The exposure and targeted advertising may be worth it. With a private line, you will save money but will be giving up the exposure.

__ **ANSWERING MACHINE.** If the office consists of you alone, this is standard equipment so you do not miss important business calls. Carefully check into features because some answering machines allow you to record your own message, some messages are prerecorded and impersonal. Many machines have a counter that tells you how many calls came in while you were out. Decide which features are important to you and be sure you compare features. Another option is a 24-hour answering service.

Tip: The police say burglars checking out house occupancy, feel that an answering machine saying, "I'm not home to take your call . . ." is an open invitation. Instead, when you record your message, say, "I can't come to the phone right now. . . ." Do not ever tell anyone when you are *not* going to be home.

__ **ELECTRONIC VOICE MAIL** (sometimes referred to as Voice Bank). Voice Bank is a computer system that provides friendly prompts to callers, enabling them to leave recorded messages in their own voices regardless of the time of day. You can even call-forward after-hours calls to your voice mailbox. With this service all calls are answered on the first attempt. Messages are time-stamped and stored for your review. You can retrieve your messages from any Touch Tone phone, using a password you select. Or, the service can alert your pager or other telephone number when calls are received. You can locate the mailboxes on your premises or the service's.

__ **TYPEWRITER.** Check into rebuilt versus a brand-new machine to save money. My suggestion is *never* be without a typewriter. Think of the image you are presenting to your clients if you are handwriting correspondence, invoices, or paperwork. Reconditioned machine prices now allow you to purchase an electronic typewriter with some memory for about the price of a new electric. If you use a typewriter only rarely, consider a portable rather than one that takes up permanent space.

___ **COMPUTER.** Do some research. It is not the computer that makes the difference, it's the software. Buy a computer that is IBM compatible (known as "clones") and you are always safe because the software will always be available. IBM has a new PS-2 line of computers well worth checking out. Model 25 is actually designed for special home use. It is a scaled-down model of the PC and has a self-contained screen and disk drive all in one.

___ **SOFTWARE.** Buy one or two basic software programs and find access to *Public Domain Software* for the rest of your software needs. This is software that programmers give away or sell for under five dollars per disk. How do you find the Public Domain Software? They are available at your local library or college library in a catalog called Demo Diskette/Public Domain. These *demo diskettes* (listed by subject) provide versions of commercially produced software that offers you a chance to examine a program prior to purchase from a commercial vendor. They are complete programs not protected by copyright laws and *may be freely duplicated.* Check with your interlibrary loan service.

Get involved with a user support group to find out what various software does. By discussing it with others, you will find out about the good and the bad programs. If you have ever visited a software store you know it can take hours of reading each software package to figure out what features each has. Instead, network and ask questions.

___ **PRINTER.** Are you aware that there are some typewriters that double as printers? If your printer will not be in constant use or speed is not a factor, these printer-typewriters are an excellent buy, not to mention saving the space of having both a typewriter and a separate printer.

Before purchasing a daisy wheel printer or dot-matrix, check into the new low-cost laser printers. Be sure you ask to see a printed page of each to see if you like the clarity of whichever type printer you choose.

___ **COPIER.** There are scaled-down versions of copiers available on the market that save space and are ideal for home offices. Cannon has a small cartridge model available for the desktop that is excellent. DAK has a desktop model that is 16 inches wide, 14½ inches deep, and 4¼ inches tall. Many of these machines are noise-free and even maintenance-free. Forget powders, toners, and drum cleaning. They are thermal copiers. Just turn these copiers on and enjoy making copies whenever and wherever you want. You may even want to check into Silver Reed's Hand Held Porta Copy (cordless) which you can carry with you in your briefcase.

__ **FILE CABINET.** Choices range from the two-drawer to four-drawer tall ones; and from the normal stand-up vertical files to drawers that open horizontally. Unless you have a large area, chances are you will not have room for the horizontal type. If your office space is limited, choose the regular two-drawer vertical cabinet. The four-drawer might be overwhelming for your room. Bobbi Moore, an image consultant, told me she chose the two-drawer files because they double as extra counter space and soften the look of the room. Set a lamp, in and out trays, or books on top of the cabinets.

Tip: If you purchase file cabinets the same color as the wall, your room will appear larger. For instance, with off-white walls, choosing an off-white cabinet will make the cabinet seem to disappear. You won't feel like you have wall-to-wall furniture.

__ **DESK CHAIR.** Comfort is a necessity if your job entails long periods of sitting. Choose a chair that gives good back support. Do not skimp by buying a cheap chair. You may end up paying the money to a chiropractor instead.

OFFICE SUPPLY CHECKLIST

What is worse than not having the proper supplies at your desk when you need them? Have you ever needed a paper clip and not been able to find one? A mad search for one little postage stamp is another frustration. As soon as you have your office set up the way you want it, stop and make a list of all the supplies you will need for your desk drawers, the top of your desk, and the shelves.

When I am consulting with businesses, I discover poorly supplied desks to be a major problem. Executives and secretaries, alike, rush from their desks many times a day in search of some missing item. Be aware of how often you have to jump out of your chair or interrupt your concentration by looking for a pad of paper, tape, or scissors. Make your work area function properly by using your basic list. Take the list with you to the office supply store. Place a check mark in front of each item you need to buy.

__ Paper clips, regular and oversized
__ Pads of paper, notebook, Post-it notes
__ Clipboard. Great to use for organizing work in progress.
__ Calendar. Use either a desk or datebook style calendar. Jot down appointments and project deadlines. (*See* the section on time management in chapter 7 for tips on how to make your calendar work.)
__ Scotch tape and dispenser
__ Stapler, staples, and staple remover

__ Pens, pencils

__ Pencil sharpener, if you are an avid pencil user. There are inexpensive manual ones or fancy electric models available.

__ Rubber bands

__ Phone message pads. A necessity if you need to keep track of client calls. There are two kinds. One type is a small pad that you can tear into individual sheets. The other is a large pad with two to four perforated messages per page which include a carbon copy as a record of all calls. The carbon copies are valuable records in case of lost messages.

Tip: Never take any call without getting a full address along with the caller's name. This information will come in handy to begin a mailing list of your own when advertising a product or service. (*See* chapter 3 for more on how to develop a mailing list.)

__ Stationery and envelopes: 8½-by-11-inch plain white bond paper with #10 business envelopes.

__ Manila or padded envelopes (if you mail out thick or fragile packages)

__ Ruler

__ Scissors

__ Letter opener

__ Highlighter pens and markers in various colors

__ In/Out trays

__ Rolodex-type name and address file

__ Desk lamp and/or wall lamp. Ceiling light gives extra soft light that is easy on the eyes. Wall lamps with an adjustable arm are great!

__ Bulletin board, push pins. If you have any wall space nearby, a bulletin board is a great place to hang notes, reminders, and zip code or area code lists. Or, purchase 12-by-12-inch square stick-on pieces of cork to make whatever size board you need.

__ Carbon paper. If you do not have a computer to keep copies of business letters/documents, be sure to use carbons to always have a backup. Copyset is a brand name which gives you carbon paper and backup paper attached which is torn off and disposed of after using.

__ Dictionary. Also consider a thesaurus if you do any amount of writing or correspondence.

__ Speller Dictionary. Webster's New World Speller is a must if your spelling leaves a lot to be desired.

__ Zip Code Directory. Available from the Post Office or through D.I. Publishing, 5713 Sawtelle Blvd., Culver City, CA 90230.

__ File folders. Letter-size (for 8½-by-11 papers) are the most-used kind. For easier viewing of tabs, choose the third-cut type which are staggered.

__ Pendaflex folders and labels

__ Postage scale

___ Stamps. Always keep the appropriate postage on hand if you mail regularly.

___ Wastebasket. A large one to hold junk mail or for when you clean out files.

___ Correction fluid. Regular and "just for copies." Correction fluid also comes in colors. Colored ones are great for mistakes on colored invoice copies.

Shop and compare office suppliers periodically. Don't just assume the one you buy from one time also has the best price the next time. Usually you can save by purchasing items through a mail order catalog. Compare prices. Here are some resources that will send you a free catalog:

Quill Corporation—100 S. Schelter Road, Lincolnshire, IL 60197-4700
Reliable—1001 W. Van Buren Street, Chicago, IL 60607
The Drawing Board—256 Regal Row, Dallas, TX 75222

A complete list of others can be found in your library in the reference book *Thomas Register*.

PRINTING NEEDS

One wonderful person had the forethought to tell me not to print more than 500 of anything in the beginning. I was so thankful. After being in business only a few months, I saw several major changes I wanted to make in the copy. It can be disastrous to have such a high quantity that when your business expands, changes, or grows you are still burdened with tons of what has become "old" material. If you have to throw it away, it doesn't save you $$.

Here are some of the things you'll need to have printed:

___ Stationery and Envelopes
___ Invoices and Statements
___ Brochures and Flyers
___ Business Cards
___ Bank Checks

Tip: The more copies you print at one time, the lower your cost will be per piece. However, remember these are your first printed materials. Do not have thousands printed, because chances are you will find improvements to make as your business and your needs progress.

Check on the mailing regulations *before* you have material printed or you could be wasting time and money by printing a piece that is too large or small. Many times, the post office can give you technical details on mailing brochures, self-mailers, or business reply mailings. While you are there, check on permit numbers you may need according to the piece you are mailing and the quantity.

What Experts Should You See?

Here is a list of the people who can help you with the details of your printing needs:

Graphic Designer—	For art, design, various type styles, use of colors, film stripping, slide presentations, billboards, book covers. They can also do start-to-finish work on a brochure or flyer, if needed.
Typesetter—	For professional typing with any size or style type. Some printers also provide this service. See your Yellow Pages.
Printer—	For copying, printing stationery and envelopes, business cards, forms, and some design drawings.
Artist—	For logo or any artwork that needs to make an impact, like making transparencies or cartoons. Usually very creative people.

Here are some questions to ask to determine *who* you should hire to do the work:

1. Does the price include folding, punching holes, collating, materials, etc.?
2. What paper stock is the price based on?
3. How many chances will I get to proof the work? If changes are made at proofing time, is there an extra charge to make revisions?
4. What is the turnaround time start to finish?

A printer's capabilities depend on the equipment he has. In the past there was a great difference between the services of "quick printing" and full-service printing. Now the only difference between a quick printer and a full-service printer is the size sheets each can run on his machine. A quick printer is usually limited to print up to the 11-by-17 size. A full-service printer can print on large sheets up to 77 inches and then cut down. Check to find the best price.

Sometimes you can save money by having photocopying done by a quick printer while you wait. However, many times because they are doing it on a "rush" basis, the cost is higher than at a full-service shop. It will be worth visiting several local print shops to compare prices on printed paper goods. Several business people I know look strictly for "personal" service from their printer. Decide what is important to you.

Tip: Get to know your printer. Once you've become a regular customer, they may offer helpful suggestions, punch holes, and so on as a favor. These little extras make the difference.

Be sure you purchase matching colors of stationery and envelopes. Be realistic and reasonable. Request catalogs from The Drawing Board (800) 527-9530 or NEBS (800) 252-9226 for window envelopes, invoices, and matching stationery selections.

Acquiring a Logo

A logo is a crucial ingredient for communicating your business or service. It is a fact that people retain a visual picture much better than words. Your logo will become your trademark and people will recognize it before your name or anything else. Whether you choose a design or your signature as a logo, keep it professional. It should be clever, but not cutesy. To develop your logo:

1. You can invest money in an artist or graphics company who charges by the hour to create and draw a custom-designed logo.
2. Ask a print shop to see paste-up books. They have a tremendous selection of drawings to choose from and any design or picture can be reduced or enlarged on a copy machine for the proper size.
3. If you are creative, you can design one yourself.

Tip: Consider having your picture put on your business card, brochure, or flyer. It gives you an additional communication tool.

Business Cards Go Fast

When just starting out your home-based business, you may want to invest in less-expensive, lighter-weight stock as you realize how fast your business cards will disappear. Your business card should include your name, business name, address, phone number (do not forget the area code), and your logo.

When comparing printing prices for business cards, letterhead, and so on, inquire about using raised ink (called *thermography*) instead of flat ink. Usually the cost is less for raised ink. *Note:* If you want to be able to make copies on your letterhead paper, you will have to use flat ink; copiers will not tolerate raised ink and they cause jams in the equipment.

A business card printed on colored stock will stand out from others, or, consider using colored ink. Some smaller printers do not charge extra for colored ink *if* you ask them to run it when they are already running that color on the press. However, if yours is the only ink change for the day, they will charge $15 to $20 for press cleanup.

Tip: One thing I have learned through the years is that the *most important* thing on a business card is your telephone number with the area code. All the rest is meaningless if your phone number isn't large enough to be seen easily. Many people make the mistake of placing a tiny phone number down in the corner. Remember, people will not strain to find their glasses in order to read your phone number. They will call someone else.

If you have a service-type business, you will want to spell out just *exactly what the service is.* If you have a tangible product to sell, try to mention, if possible, what the product is or does (*see* page 46, "Choosing a Business Name," for more on this). Here are some sample business cards:

Service-type business   Product-type business

Your business cards can only help you if you hand them out freely. Leave them everywhere possible for exposure.

Tip: I found some restaurants, delis, printers, and beauty salons that allow me to place my cards and/or brochures on their counters. Several new business clients have resulted.

An excellent source of advertisement is the display space available *free* at your local chamber of commerce. Most chambers are eager to help small businesses because businesses improve the community.

3

Growing Your Business

TO GET A GOOD, SOLID START for your business, you *must* have certain facts and a plan to follow. Here is a step-by-step checklist for you to use. This information will be helpful in many ways, from applying for a business loan or setting marketing goals to obtaining a business counselor. Take the time to do this for yourself so you will always have the pertinent information at your fingertips. You will find yourself referring to this checklist again and again.

Checklist for Starting Up Your Own Business

Today's Date: _____   Target Date for Starting My Business: _____

Action to Be Taken	Target Date	Date Done
1. Obtain a copy of my personal credit report	_____	_____
2. Complete my personal financial statement	_____	_____
3. Create or update my personal résumé (a necessity if applying for a loan)	_____	_____
4. Write a description of my business that can be understood by *anyone*	_____	_____
5. Write my marketing and advertising plan	_____	_____
6. Write my overall business plan	_____	_____
7. Obtain a professional small business counselor	_____	_____
8. Obtain an "informal" or "credit card" line of credit	_____	_____
9. Develop a "formal" line of credit	_____	_____
10. Decide on the best legal form of business to use (sole proprietorship, partnership, or corporation)	_____	_____
11. Decide on my business name	_____	_____
12. Obtain a "certificate of ownership"	_____	_____
13. Open a separate business checking account	_____	_____
14. Decide on any extra insurance I will need	_____	_____
15. Obtain any business licenses required	_____	_____
16. Obtain a sales tax number (if needed)	_____	_____
17. Develop a "banking relationship"	_____	_____
18. Borrow early and finance long-term	_____	_____

START WITH A BUSINESS PLAN

Writing a Business Plan is required in order to:

1. Start a new business
2. Guide an existing business
3. Obtain loan financing
4. Attract investors

The most thorough information on developing a business plan I have ever found (and the easiest to understand) comes from a former banker, Frank Hackathorn of Dallas. He has had his own home-based business consulting practice since 1983. He designed this outline especially for small businesses.

Business Plan Outline

- **Cover**
  - A. Name of business
  - B. Name and title of principal(s)
  - C. Address of business
  - D. Phone number of business

- **Non-Disclosure Agreement**
  - A. This document is the property of _____
  - B. Importance of confidentiality
  - C. Photocopying or sharing information prohibited
  - D. Not an offer to sell stock, etc.

- **Statement of Purpose**
  - A. To start a new business
  - B. To guide an existing business
  - C. To obtain loan financing
  - D. To attract investors
    (choose one and explain it in no more than half a page)

- **Table of Contents**
1. **Executive Summary**
   - A. Most important part to bankers and investors
   - B. No more than 2 to 4 pages long
   - C. Not done until plan is completely written
   - D. Very brief summations of each section of the plan
   - E. Most difficult part of plan to do correctly

2. **Loan Request** (applicable if purpose of plan is to obtain loan financing)
   - A. Request (company name, legal form, wishes to borrow $_____)
   - B. Amount(s) and term(s) (money wanted and time needed to pay it back)

   C. Repayment schedule(s) (payment(s) to be made monthly, quarterly, annually, etc.)

   D. Purpose of loan(s) (how the money will be used)

   E. Source(s) of repayment (initial source and secondary source if necessary)

   F. Collateral and value (description and current market value of collateral)

   G. Conditions (providing financial statements, insurance, personal guarantees, etc.)

3. Banking Plan (applicable if purpose of plan is to obtain loan financing)

   A. Banking relationship objective

   B. Account relationship intentions

   C. Potential business accounts

   D. Potential personal accounts

4. Company Description

   A. Name and legal form of business

   B. Description of location and facilities

   C. Date formed and brief history

   D. Mission statement (purpose for existence)

      1. *Who* is being satisfied (customer groups)
      2. *What* is being satisfied (customer needs)
      3. *How* customer needs are satisfied (technologies)

   E. Any other general information that is pertinent

5. Products or Services

   A. Description of products or services

   B. Major features and major benefits

   C. Proprietary position: copyrights, trademarks, patents, and legal and technical considerations

   D. Comparison to competitors' products and services

6. Manufacturing Process (if applicable)

   A. Materials and costs

   B. Labor and costs

   C. Sources of supply

   D. Pricing strategies and policy

   E. Methods of producing, selling, distributing, and servicing products

7. Management and Personnel

   A. Personal history of the principals

   B. Related work experience of the principals

   C. Salary, duties, and responsibilities of management

   D. Salary, duties, and responsibilities of personnel

    E. Outside resources available (consultants, specialists, etc.)

    F. Type of banking specialists available (or needed)

8. Goals and Strategies

    A. Research information

    B. Set goals

    C. Create objectives

    D. Plan strategies

    E. Action plan

    F. Results monitoring system

9. Market Environment

    A. Your target market

    B. Geographic area of your market

    C. Description of the total market

    D. Your current and your desired market share

    E. Degree of competitiveness in market

    F. Industry trends

    G. Current economic conditions

10. Competition

    A. Identifying the competition

    B. Investigating the competition

    C. Analyzing the competition

    D. Identifying your competitive edge

11. Marketing Plan

    A. Products or services definition

    B. Identifying uniqueness

    C. Target market definition

    D. Define their wants

    E. Goals, objectives, and strategies

    F. Marketing budget

    G. Action plan

    H. Results monitoring system

12. Financial Data

    A. Financial statements (fiscal year-end for five years to present)

    B. Five-year financial projections (1st year monthly, 2nd & 3rd years quarterly, 4th & 5th years annually)

        1. Balance sheets

        2. Income statements

        3. Cash flow

        4. Capital expenditure estimates

    C. Explanation of projections

    D. Explanation of use and effect of new funds

   E. Potential return to investors (applicable if purpose of plan is to attract
        investors)

13. Supporting Documents
   A. Any legal document relevant to your business
   B. Price quotes or bids on leasehold improvements
   C. Patents, copyrights, trademarks, contracts, or leases
   D. Letters of intent to do business with you
   E. Letters of reference from people who know you
   F. A current credit report on yourself
   G. Personal résumés and letters of recommendation
   H. Industry studies, census, or demographic data
   I. Insurance requirements and license requirements
   J. Copies of brochures, flyers, direct mail pieces, etc.
   K. Copies of any favorable publicity for business, public service, or civic
        awards you or your business have received if relevant to your business
   L. Anything else that you feel is important to show how your business can
        be successful

EXPENSES, DEDUCTIONS, AND INSURANCE

Start-up Expenses

Take the time to make a list of your start-up expenses to get an idea of how
much money you will need to invest or request for a business loan. Here is a
basic-needs list to which you can add other items your particular type of
business may require:

Business license or permit	$ _____
Equipment and installation	_____
Remodeling and decorating	_____
Advertising/Marketing	_____
Professional or legal fees	_____
Office inventory	_____
Printing needs	_____
Business checking account	_____
_____	_____
_____	_____
TOTAL	$ _____

Choosing a Business Name

One of the best business tips someone shared with me is to name your business
something that says exactly what you do. It can have a tremendous effect on

your success. You will have a head start if the name of your business explains your product or services. A company called Sam's or Johnny's is really gambling on the chance that people care enough to find out what kind of business it is. How about one called Perfect Inventory? Your guess is as good as mine as to what kind of business it is. Think about how much more business they would do if their name explained their occupation like Sam's Catalog Furniture, Johnny's Plumbing, or Perfect Fashion Inventory.

Tip: Communicating precisely what your business is and does can mean everything. It's hard enough to start up a new business without putting yourself at a disadvantage by the name you choose. This name is your "handle" and what clients will remember.

Registering Your Business

This means getting your permit to do business. When you've chosen your business name, you must obtain a Certificate of Ownership, by going in person to your city hall. You will need to check through microfilm they keep on file to be sure there is not already a business with the same name. If you choose your proper name as part of your company name, i.e., Smith and Associates, you won't need to go through this procedure, but still need to ask about a Business Permit. The cost for these will be approximately ten dollars, although I understand it is higher in some cities.

Will You Be Selling a Product? You will need to visit your comptroller's office and make an application for a Sales and Use Tax Permit. The number they issue to you will be used for any supplies or merchandise purchased for resale to eliminate paying taxes at that particular time. When the product is sold, you collect tax and set it aside to send in with your quarterly tax report mailed to you from your State Comptroller of Public Accounts.

What Type of Business?

You will need to decide how your Certificate of Ownership will be classified: sole proprietorship, partnership, or corporation.

Sole Proprietorship—a business owned by one person. It is not incorporated. Your business may have many employees or you may be the only person.

Partnership—owned by two or more persons but still unincorporated. The partnership agreement is a legal relation existing between two or more persons who have contracted to place money, effects, labor, and skill to do business together with the understanding that they will share the profits between them.

There are *limited* partnerships that have one or more general partners and one or more *limited partners*. The legal definition of a limited partner is a partner whose liability to creditors of the partnership is limited to the amount of capital he has contributed to the partnership, providing he has not held himself out to the public as a general partner and has complied with other requirements of the law.

There are also *general* partnerships where one is held to resemble another partner in having joint rights and responsibilities.

Corporation—a business that is incorporated and which observes state laws and regulations.

Joint Venture—a business enterprise of speculative nature.

Whether you are applying for a loan, a tax permit, or even applying for credit from an office supply store, you will always be asked what type of business it is for government records. Once you decide which way your business will be classified, remember, it is not set in stone. You can make an additional application later, if you decide to change your status.

Your U.S. Small Business Administration Office is your best resource on how to write a business plan, apply for a loan, or for financial advice. The S.B.A. will also mail you booklets about starting your home-based business upon request. Some are free and some are available for a nominal cost. Call and ask them to send you a list of information available.

In Canada there is no government-run resource or association for small businesses. There is, however, the Small Business Network, Inc., which teaches classes on how to start and maintain a small business. You can contact them at 2180 Steele's Avenue W., Suite 216, Concord, Ontario, Canada L4K 2Z5.

Tax Information and Deductions

When you are self-employed, it is important to learn the facts about what expenses you can claim and what taxes must be paid. Find an accountant to tell you exactly what can be deducted on April 15. The Self-Employment Form to use is Schedule C, Form 1040. *Note:* You *must make estimated quarterly payments* of income and self-employment tax. Otherwise, you will have to pay a penalty to the IRS. Marc Core, CPA, filled me in on some income tax specifics you should know.

Always obtain the advice of your own tax advisor before making any tax-related decisions. The laws have become very complicated and are subject to change. Here are some general guidelines:

House Deductions. If you use a portion of your home "exclusively" for conducting business, then you can claim deductions for an office in the home. This means that it cannot also be used as a guest room when Aunt Rose comes for a visit. What can be claimed as deductions? A percentage (number of square feet in the office divided by the number of square feet in your home) of utilities, repairs, maintenance, telephone, mortgage interest, real estate taxes, insurance, and depreciation.

Tip: Most people don't realize that deducting the home in-office portion of interest and real estate taxes on Schedule C will lower self-employment tax even though it won't have any effect on the amount of income tax.

To depreciate a portion of the house, you need to know:

1. What you paid for the house
2. How much you have spent on improvements
3. The value of the land (or an estimate of its value) when you purchased the home

Remember that you depreciate your cost, *not the value* when you open your office. You *cannot* depreciate land.

	Original Cost
+	Cost of Improvements
−	Cost of Land
=	Tax Basis of Your Home
×	Office in Home Percentage
=	Amount You May Depreciate

Consult your tax advisor or IRS publications for the proper rates to apply in order to determine the amount of depreciation you can deduct in any one year.

If you take depreciation, what happens when you sell that home? Any additional depreciation (that is, depreciation greater than what would have been taken on a regular, straight-line basis) is subject to being "recaptured" as ordinary income when you sell the home. That will raise your taxes in the year of sale. There may be other tax consequences of selling your home about which you should consult your tax advisor.

Car Expenses. Business mileage divided by total number of miles driven for the year is your business-use percentage allowed. You may deduct this percentage of your total auto cost including gas, oil, repairs, insurance, interest, and licenses. Your records must reflect the total miles driven for the year and you *must* keep a complete and accurate log of your business mileage in order to prove your deduction.

Visit your local office supply store and check out the wide selection of auto expense record books to help you keep good records. Each time you drive anywhere that is business related, enter your beginning mileage and your ending mileage. Parking, trips to the post office, tolls, and tips are also included in some of the auto expense books. Keeping track of all your car expenses in one book saves time and frustration.

Entertainment and Meals. Rules regarding meals and entertainment are very strict. You must keep complete records reflecting *where, what, who, how much,* and *why* for each expenditure. You can deduct 80 percent of your business meals and entertainment costs.

Jot down a note on your meal receipt that explains the who, when, and so on. Keep an envelope in your car or briefcase and slip the meal receipts into this "special" envelope. This will make it easy to find at the end of the month. If you keep receipts quarterly or yearly, rather than monthly, you will want to use folders with each month designated.

Office Expenses. You are allowed up to $10,000 of capital equipment expense each year. This deduction must be taken in the year the expenditure was made. Otherwise, the capital item is depreciated over a specified number of years. If you sell or dispose of equipment before it would have been fully depreciated, then you will "recapture" a prorated amount of the deduction as additional income in the year of disposal.

Want an easy way to keep track of expenses and receipts? One home-based businessman told me he keeps all his receipts in an expandable folder, labeled by month. He slips the receipts into the current month and has all the information at his fingertips for end-of-the-year reports.

How to Find an Accountant

There are two different kinds of accountants you can choose from who can do the job for you.

Public Accountants may, or may not, be extremely knowledgeable. They have not passed a standardized, rigorous exam and are not regulated by any state authority.

Certified Public Accountants also may, or may not, be extremely knowledgeable. However, they have passed a two-and-one-half-day standardized rigorous exam and are generally required to complete a certain number of continuing education hours each year. Depending on the state, they also have at least 30 academic hours of accounting. CPA's are regulated by the state.

Interview your accountant as thoroughly as you would an employee you might hire. Ask questions about an accountant's education and experience. Get a feel for his expertise. Shop around and choose one you feel comfortable with and who best fills your needs. Then you can make an educated decision.

If you find yourself totally confused,
DON'T CRY . . .
You understand the situation better
than you think!

Insurance Coverage

Beware! Each state has its own regulations, policies, and coverages on home-based offices. The rates on additional coverage depend on whether you use equipment in the home (on premises) only or if you travel (off premises) with the equipment. A normal homeowner's policy automatically covers $2,500 of office and business equipment used on premises only. But, if you have invested heavily in computers, typewriters, copy machines, or nice office furniture, you may need additional coverage in the form of an endorsement rider.

For example, in Texas, if you have more than $2,500 worth of office and business equipment you need to add an endorsement that will cover up to $8,000 at a cost of $40 per year, as quoted by a State Farm agent. This covers you *on* and *off* the premises in case you haul the computer around or take the calculator in the car or to another office.

If you are an engineer, independent real estate agent, computer operator, or a consultant who has people coming into the home, you may need to add an Incidental Office Occupancy policy. This is a commercial business policy. *Be sure you consult your insurance agent as to eligibility for coverage specific to your needs.* Remember, it doesn't cost a thing to ask questions.

**SELLING Is a Little Like Hog Calling . . .
It Isn't the NOISE You Make —
It's the APPEAL in Your Voice!**

CREATE MARKETING AND SALES STRATEGIES

What methods will you use to sell your product or service? Will telemarketing, direct-mail marketing, cold calling, or media be the best route to take? And, what type of sales strategies are you most comfortable with? Some people consider cold calling a challenge and others hate it. Do not use strategies that make you uncomfortable. If you are trying to develop a new strategy, practice in front of the mirror or with a friend. Then ask for feedback. Practice until you are confident or your inexperience will show.

What sales technique is best to use? How you sell your service or product to each prospective buyer is strictly personal preference. Using the same technique with each customer you contact will *not* work. You will develop various strategies as you discover each customer has to be handled as an individual. Some will require a harder sell than others, and some customers will only buy with a softer sell technique. Your intuition and common sense should rule in sales situations. This is why selling is such an art.

How can this art be learned? With a watchful eye, study other salespeople who sell a product or service to you. What did you like about what they said or did? What turned you off? In studying other sales methods, remember what you do not like in a salesperson is usually what other people don't like either. One rule of thumb to follow is to BE HONEST! For example, when a salesperson says, "I will have that available for you in two days," and it turns out to be two weeks, he loses credibility.

People who break sales records often will tell you they are honest with the customer. It is the only way to win trust and respect. Customers are understanding when a regrettable situation occurs *if* it is explained, but they turn bitter when the truth is twisted or when they are given flimsy excuses.

Why can one person sell a service or product that the next person cannot? Because the successful salesperson fills a need and provides a service that is superior to what his competition offers. Study your competitor and his weakness and use this information to your benefit.

Making Proposals

At one time or another, whether you are selling a product or a service, you will need to make a proposal to generate or close the sale. Here are some various ideas for using proposals:

One-on-One Proposal. When making a marketing proposal in person, always give a potential client an outline of what you believe the problem is and how you can solve it. Your success will depend on *what* you say and *how* you say it. When meeting with a decision maker one-on-one you need to make a mental checklist of these items:

1. Always *prepare* ahead what you will say, and *think* first before talking.
2. *Listen* closely to what the client needs.
3. Use *visual aids* when possible to hold the client's attention and to put variety into your presentation.

4. *Speak* simply without using impressive words or terminology that is confusing. Pronounce words properly, be aware of your *voice* speed, tone, and volume for best results.

Mail Proposal. When you communicate with a written proposal, it is important that you follow some specifics to increase your effectiveness because your professional image is on the line. Use a brief, to-the-point letter and follow it up with a phone call. In the letter tell the clients that you will be following up on a certain date and look forward to speaking with them about your proposal. (Be sure you *do* call them at the time you stated in the letter.) If you don't get their attention in the first few lines, they won't bother reading any further. When writing a proposal, follow these simple guidelines:

1. Ask yourself what the *purpose* of the letter will be.
2. Organize a quick *outline* so you don't wander off the subject.
3. Use *short* sentences. Try to write just like you talk so the feel of the letter is personal, not disconnected and cold.
4. Is the proposal organized and easy to read and understand?
5. Did you spell out the benefits to the client?
6. Do you sound confident and knowledgeable?
7. Did you cover the client's needs?
8. Did you read the proposal from your client's standpoint?
9. Are the grammar, spelling, and sentence structure correct?
10. Did you set a specific time to follow up?
11. Do you have a cover letter to send with the proposal?
12. Be sure to PROOFREAD your letter before sending it. (If you cannot be objective about your own writing, have a friend, spouse, or secretary proof it for you.) This seemingly minor routine is *critical* whether you are selling a service or a product. How well you present yourself through written work can make the difference between turning the client *off* or *on*.

At one time or another, we have all received written communication that turned us off. Recently, a friend of mine received a brochure from a person who was promoting his business of writing and producing brochures for others businesses. At first glance his brochure was very impressive until several spelling errors were discovered in the content. Would you want this person to do a brochure for you?

Flyer/Brochure Proposal. Another form for a proposal is a flyer or brochure. These can be very professionally and inexpensively done with software that is available today like DeskTop Publishing, or you can have them typeset and printed.

Tip: Make your brochure a self-mailer by having one panel for name and address. It saves money because you do not need an envelope.

Telemarketing

Determine what you offer in your business that no one else does. In other words, what is unique about your product or service? Make a list of all the people you know, and call to tell them about your home-based business and how your services will be beneficial to them. Realize that telemarketing takes "many" calls to close the sale. This is common as far as telemarketing goes. Eighty percent of all sales are made after five calls. However, only 10 percent of all salespeople keep persisting after the fifth contact. Have perseverance and watch your sales percentages increase.

When the Contact Says No

Don't give up if a contact says no. Instead, ask if you can mail them information for future needs. Send a thank-you letter to say how much you appreciated their time. Enclose a flyer, catalog, or even a proposal explaining how you can fill their needs. Then, call back in six months and start all over again. Most of all, don't get discouraged. Your enthusiasm is projected through your voice and attitude, so don't let them hear your disappointment. Remember to visualize yourself succeeding and think positive!

Planning is the most useful tool you own for great telemarketing. Write out a script of what you want to say when you reach the marketing contact. *Do not read* the script. Just write it out and study it for a couple of minutes before picking up the phone. Use a Post-it note tacked up on the bulletin board in front of you with questions or points you want to make during the conversation. Make calls from a list in front of you that includes *who* you are going to call on and why. Then, set aside enough time to work on your plan.

Tip: Prevent clients from catching you off guard. When customers call you to negotiate prices for a service, they take you by surprise. Whenever you can, ask if you may call them back. Get your ducks in a row by checking files for information you may need to handle the conversation. This way you are more prepared to deal with the negotiation because *you* have the advantage. A fellow speaker I know told me that he never begins negotiation when receiving the initial call. He always asks to call them back so he is ready with proper information.

Turn leads into sales by developing a good follow-up plan. Use a calendar, tickler file, or three-by-five-inch cards to keep track of prospects' contact dates and their responses. Each time a prospect asks you to check back later, whether next week or next year, jot it down on a specific date so you don't forget and end up missing a possible opportunity.

What to Do When Your Phone Stops Ringing

Now that you are in business for yourself, the phone is your lifeline. It can be scary and frustrating when it *stops* ringing. Take inventory when this happens to find out what may be wrong.

- Are you marketing on a regular basis? Set aside specific days or times each week to develop new contacts or update established accounts.
- Are you keeping your name in front of the customers by letting them know when you have *new* products or *new* services available?
- Do you follow up after the sale? Are you asking customers for feedback to be sure you are meeting their needs?
- Is your answering service or recording machine dependable so you aren't missing any messages?
- Are you returning calls? Don't neglect giving this special and important touch.

Once you discover the weak link, concentrate on correcting the problem. Set aside time each week to find new clients. Whether you market by phone or in person, *do it regularly*. If you do not market on a regular basis, a few months down the road the lack of business catches up to you. Keep building business! It's easy to fall prey to getting too involved in the daily work and not lining up future work. Do not relax your marketing strategies when business is good. The sense of "being busy right now" overpowers the need to take time to continually market. Keep tomorrow, next week, or next month's business in mind. The idea is to keep your phone ringing with either new sales or repeat sales.

One home-business owner sums it up saying, "Marketing and sales are the keys to developing your business." The first thing you need to know is where the market is for your product or service. You market with the sale in mind because nothing happens until the sale is made. So, unless you are just plain lucky, you will waste time *and* money if you don't know exactly *who* needs your product or service. Here's a checklist to help you identify your market for advertising and promotion:

_____	Organizations	_____	Small Businesses
_____	Corporations	_____	Associations
_____	Retail Stores	_____	Wholesale Distributors
_____	The Public	_____	Other
_____	Government Agencies (city or state)		

Once you know what market to focus on, break it down even further: what ages, what income level, men, women, college students, etc. Even if you intend to market to all of the above, it is very expensive to market every segment at one time. Prioritize your markets as you budget your advertising dollar so you will be investing your money to give you back the highest return.

Creative, innovative advertising has proven to be the best kind. Use your imagination to think of new and clever ways to gain attention in your advertising. One consultant who works out of her home told me she learned it was a "waste" of money to advertise her service-type business in newspapers. Since a service business is intangible, it requires a different type of advertising than selling a retail product. The consultant fared better spending money to advertise in trade publications and directly to the businesses who use her consulting services.

WAYS TO ADVERTISE

Here are some marketing ideas to help promote your *service-type* business:

Display Ads in business or trade journals. Keep the ad clean and simple, not cluttered with too many words. Use a phrase that tells the readers how they will benefit from using your service, or ask a question that "grabs" the readers.

Showcase/Exhibits in trade shows where you can display your service. For the cost of a booth, you can promote your business and schedule appointments. Showcases that fit your industry are, of course, the most beneficial. You can investigate available trade shows at the library, the chamber of commerce, or through business organizations you belong to. Many business organizations even participate in trade shows each year.

Some questions to ask them before deciding to exhibit:

• Is there a registration fee?
• What is the profile of the attendees?
• How many have attended in the past? How many are expected at this one?
• Will you be able to sell products or only services?

Here are some ideas to help you get the most mileage from an exhibit space:

1. Attract people to stop at your booth. When setting up your booth area, use an attention-getter that people can see across the room. A catchy display with splashy colors, a creative twist, or using big letters helps make an impact.
2. Keep visitors at your booth and focused on your business as long as possible. Try having them take a quick test that reveals their need for your service, or have them guess the number of marbles in a bottle or watch themselves on a VCR or talk to a robot.
3. Collect business cards by having a drawing for a prize. This way you gain new prospect lists. Qualify inquiries by getting enough information to decide if they are good potential customers.
4. Always give them something to take home as a reminder of your business. Try an item with your business name and phone number: a pen, a magnet, a money-off coupon (if they call you within 30 days), a brochure, or interesting reading material.

Organization Directories. Organizations that you belong to usually allow you to advertise your service at a very reasonable price. Place a business card ad or a quarter-page ad to let members know exactly what service you provide. Include your picture in the ad for additional interest.

Newsletter Publications. Service-type businesses can generate clients by looking for individuals/businesses who publish newsletters. Many times they will let you advertise FREE in their monthly publications. They may mail to a specific area in the city or even distribute their newsletters nationally. The exposure is fantastic and it doesn't cost a dime! (For information on how to develop your own newsletter, see the section in this chapter on "Writing a Newsletter to Increase Business.")

Tip: If the producer of the newsletter *does* want to charge you an advertising fee, try negotiating to trade services. Offer to write an article for the newsletter if they will run your ad at no cost.

To advertise a *product-type* business consider these possibilities:

Classified Newspaper Ads. Visit your local newspaper office to inquire about advertising rates. The key here is to *ask for help*. They want you to get good results so you will continue to advertise with them. The newspaper representatives can be very helpful. They will assist you in placing your ad in the section where it will get the best results. For instance, if you have a water-purification system, you would want to place the ad in the health section. They will also inform you of any "special theme editions" they have coming up that allow greater exposure for your particular business.

Telephone Book. White-Page advertising is by company name. Yellow-Page advertising is purchased by the block and called a space ad. You pay for the particular size space you wish to fill.

Direct Mail. This needs to be done as an ongoing process, not a one-shot approach. Direct-mail marketing has to be done on a consistent basis. Every month or every three months is not too often. Some direct-mail services believe in mailing each week for an allotted length of time. After mailing over and over, you must follow up with phone calls to make it work.

Send out letters, brochures, cards, or coupons to specific markets. Use first-class mail to get the best response. Postcards make a super mailing piece as they can be read quickly. Other people along the way also tend to read them. Reply cards that are perforated work well. Use bullets, arrows, asterisks, or check marks to direct the reader's eye. Never send a flyer or brochure by itself. *Always* include a cover letter. Use powerful words like *proven, tested, money, health,* or *education.*

Magazine Ads. This is a more expensive route to take. You are charged for space according to the magazine's circulation. Naturally, the more people the magazine reaches, the more expensive the ad.

Catalog Advertising. This means of promotion becomes more popular as people become busier and more time conscious. Produce a catalog if you have several products. Have organized photographs and descriptions of products with prices and an order form. *Note:* Don't forget to list a separate charge to cover your postage and handling expenses.

Showcase Exhibits (*see* information under advertising a service). Before you purchase a booth or space be sure you are allowed to promote your product and also take orders or sell on-site.

Take every opportunity to meet and get to know people in the news media. Do some research by calling your local newspaper, radio, or television station. After your initial phone call check back periodically with your contact and follow up with a press release or a press kit.

News Releases. A news release (also referred to as a *press release*) gives the press information about your business. This is a *free* method of advertising but also risky because you never know for sure if the newspaper will print your release. However, it doesn't cost you much for a brief typed release and a postage stamp. You might use this type of advertising to announce:

- a new product or service
- obtaining a new customer whose name people would recognize
- an award or anniversary you want to highlight

For instance, when your home business is established, have a picture taken and made into a four-by-five black-and-white glossy. Write a brief story about yourself, your background, and what is different about your business. In the story, state your business objectives too.

Tip: Reprint any publicity stories and news releases that appear. These give you credibility and are a great source of advertising to use as mailers or handouts.

Be prepared to send news releases again and again. Newspapers say *do not call.* They will print it when and if they are ready. Address your release to the editor to have the best chance of getting it in the paper. Investigate to find out what newspapers like to receive in a press release. I called the largest newspaper office in my city and asked. Here's what they told me a news release should contain:

1. Format should be typed, double-spaced, with one- to two-inch-wide margins.

2. Answer these questions in the release: how, when, who, what, where, and why.
3. Keep it brief, but thorough, with facts not fluff.
4. Put your logo and the name of your business on it to show you are a professional.
5. Be sure your phone number is on the release as a contact for more information.
6. If you submit a picture, be sure it is a black-and-white glossy. To send news releases to radio and TV stations, follow this same procedure. They don't often announce news releases, but on a slow news day when they look for news to fill time, you may find yourself getting *free* publicity.

Here is a sample news release:

News Release
For release on: <u>Wednesday, Oct.12</u>

MEDIA CONTACT:	Sharon Carr 416-1677
NEWS RELEASE:	American Businesswomen's Club
MEETING:	First Thursday of each month
DATE:	Next Meeting: October 22, 1988
TIME:	7:00 A.M.–8:00 A.M.
PLACE:	Brookhaven Country Club
COST:	Lunch buffet: $7.00 for guests
PROGRAM:	"Strategies for Managing Stress"
SPEAKER:	Sharon Carr from "Time" of Your Life
RESERVATIONS:	Betty Smith 416-7253
	No reservation needed
	Guests are always welcome.

Sharon Carr, who will give the October 22 program for the American Business-women's Club, is a Speaker and Consultant on SELF-MANAGEMENT for businesses, colleges, associations, and churches. In her message on "Strategies for Managing Stress," she will tell how she conquered a stress disease and transformed her life from one of high stress and low self-esteem to one of peace, happiness, and health.

For more information on news releases, invest seven dollars in *How to Write and Use Simple Press Releases That Work*, by Kate Kelly, Visibility Enterprises, 450 West End Avenue, New York, NY 10024. It not only contains guidelines for how to write releases but also has a media resource directory.

Press Kits. Sending a press kit can be very effective when attempting to reach the media about your product or service. A press kit is a package (folder) that contains a press release and fact sheet. It can also contain a brochure, profile of your company or personnel, news clippings, reference letters, photographs, etc. Like a press release, a press kit needs to be sent more than one time in most cases unless you have contacted the media people in advance and they are expecting it.

DEVELOPING A MAILING LIST

Have you noticed there is a mail explosion going on in this country? If you don't believe it, just keep track of the amount of advertising you receive in the mail in a one-week period.

How can you use mail to benefit your business? First of all, you need to develop a mailing list by collecting client information on a regular basis. Mail is an effective way to reach customers. Every person who shows interest in you or your service or product is a potential mailing list contact. Why develop a mailing list?

1. To keep in touch with customers
2. To do test marketing
3. To get feedback
4. To build a client base
5. To revive inactive accounts
6. To build goodwill
7. To announce new product lines

You may even want to keep several different mailing lists. One will be a *General Mailing List* of interested businesses or individuals who have requested a catalog, a sample, a brochure or quote, or other information. Keep another list of *Customers* who have actually bought from you or used your services. For example, I keep a list of everyone who attends my programs for my general mailing list and another for people who actually purchase cassettes, books, or newsletters subscriptions. This tells me who the buyers are that support me. They are great prospects for future products and services I will offer.

Above all, keep your mailing lists current by updating them periodically. What are your best sources for collecting names for a mailing list?

- Current customers
- Sales receipts or invoices
- Membership lists
- Past customers
- Shipping records
- Questionnaires/surveys

Buying a List

Want to buy an existing list? Call a mailing service or list broker to request and purchase a specific group of names. Say that you want to target a specific market such as lawyers and real estate offices. For a fee of $35 to $50 per thousand names, you can buy either a list with a contact name and phone number or a list of labels already addressed. If you do buy the already-addressed labels, be sure to ask that they be addressed to a specific title: Personnel Director, Product Manager, CEO, Hospital Administrator, and so on. This way you will increase your chances of reaching the decision maker. A list broker usually requires a minimum order of 5,000 names. The mailing list companies are responsible for keeping the lists, addresses, and contact people up-to-date. The time and research you save is worth the investment when you have a target group to reach.

A mailing list can be crucial to generate or qualify leads, provide information about your product or service, or solicit orders. The experts say to receive good response from direct mail you must mail between five and seven times. Mailing every 60 to 90 days is the best lapse time. A 2 percent response on a 100-piece mailing is considered a good return. So, don't get discouraged!

Are there better times of the year to do mail marketing? Yes! Think about your product and when it will make the greatest impact or fill the greatest need. If it is a year-round product or service, one of the best times of the year to mail is the first of January. Also, individuals and businesses are more open and ready to buy at the beginning of a new year. Take time to plan the month(s) of the year that are the most ideal for your product or service exposure.

If you mass-mail letters or flyers send them at bulk rate rather than first class. This cost is about half of the normal postage. Purchase your bulk rate permit, about $50 per calendar year (January through December), from the post office. *Beware!* If you purchase a permit late in the year, you pay the full $50 for using it just through the end of the year. In January the annual $50 fee falls due again.

Tip: When possible, do your mail marketing using stamps rather than a postage meter. A meter sign on the envelope *cuts* response rate.

WRITE A NEWSLETTER TO INCREASE BUSINESS

Watch your business soar when you start writing and publishing your own newsletter. A newsletter is one of the most effective ways to keep in touch with customers, a great method of marketing, and a wonderful source of passive income. Begin collecting stories, cartoons, facts, or any information about your business that would interest your clients. If you are not good at writing, dictate articles or sections of the newsletter into a recorder and have a secretarial service transcribe it.

Here are some ideas to include in your newsletter:

- Interesting tips about your industry
- Information on new products or services
- Announcements of special discount programs or coupons
- Congratulations on a client's business anniversary
- List of recent clients you've obtained to give you credibility
- Articles about ways to save money, live healthier, and so on
- Order form for products you offer
- Funny quips or sayings about your industry

To obtain information about the thousands of newsletter subscriptions that are available all over the country, visit a library and check through these reference books: *Business Publication Rates and Data* and *Consumer Magazine and Farm Publication Rates and Data.* The subscription charges range from $10 to $300 a year. You can publish a newsletter monthly, quarterly, semi-annually, or whenever your time allows. This is a simple but persuasive means of marketing to prospective or longtime clients.

Tip: Ask another person whose business theme will compliment yours, to write an article for your newsletter. Or, if he produces his own newsletter, trade-off articles in each other's publications. This adds extra interest and attention.

Use the newsletter as a marketing tool, by sending it out on a regular basis to potential customers. If you are selling widgets and keep information about *your* widgets coming across a customer's desk regularly, who do you think he will call when he is ready to buy a widget?

4
Managing Your Time

You Can Save Time by Shining Only the Tops of Your Shoes

HOW DO YOU FIND WAYS to save time? You learn to manage time not only to be better organized or to get more done, but also to give yourself a better quality of life. Have you ever noticed that somehow the *have-to's* always seem to get done but there is never time left for the *want-to's?* The effective time manager finds ways to get the have-to's done by setting priorities and leaving time for the want-to's.

Did you know that if you can save just 15 minutes a day you gain 11 working days a year? What would you do with an extra 11 days? Spend more time with your family, go on a long trip, finish school to get that degree, or relax and unwind? Take it a step further and imagine saving one hour a day. This adds up to saving 44 extra working days a year. The Bible says we need to be "good stewards of time." We can use time to enhance our days by controlling the minutes, hours, and days or we can let time pass through our fingers without ever making enough time for ourselves, others, and the things we like to do. If you have ever wondered where your time goes, here are the results of a study by a time expert in Pittsburgh:

Where Does Your Time Go?

6 Years	—	Eating
5 Years	—	Standing in line
2 Years	—	Returning phone calls to people *not in*
1 Year	—	Trying to find lost things
8 Months	—	Opening junk mail
6 Months	—	Sitting at traffic lights

As a home-based business person, you will feel that time is against you. This is because you are doing everything yourself and there is so much happening so fast. Start out by forming the right time-management habits. Unfortunately, no one else can manage time for you, so let's discuss what you can do specifically to help yourself.

CONQUER THE TIME ROBBERS

What wastes time for you: the phone, interruptions, forgetting things, or finding lost papers? To conquer the time robbers in your life, you must first learn to recognize them. Knowing the causes of time loss and the solution to fighting the robbers is your strongest armor. These time robbers usually fall into four categories. Read over the Time Robber Chart to see which kind you are up against. After studying the robber that steals time from you, the cause of each robber, and the solution, be sure to fill in the benefit section. Some examples of benefits for you might be the following: to save time, money, stress, or even to save thought process. If you don't see the benefit, it won't seem worthwhile to conquer the robbers.

Time Robber	Cause	Solution	Benefits of Conquering
PROCRASTINA-TION	Indecision	Just *Begin!* Mistakes are easily corrected.	_____
DISORGANIZA-TION	Improper Planning	Get organized. Put things away. Take the time now to save time later.	_____
SPINNING WHEELS	Lack of Priorities	Decide what is important and what's not. Don't just put out fires.	_____
FORGETFUL-NESS	Mind Clutter	Write things down rather than having to remember.	_____

Procrastination

This is the worst time robber for most people. Think about something you put off day after day: phone calls, correspondence, telemarketing. Have you ever put something off for such a long time that when you finally finished it, you wondered why you didn't do it long ago because it only took a few minutes? Do things *now*. Ask yourself these questions to determine whether you are a procrastinator:

1. **Why** do I put things off? Is it lack of motivation? Am I afraid of doing it wrong? Do I fear starting?
2. **When** do I put things off? Is it usually at the beginning, in the middle, or at the end of a project?
3. **What** do I procrastinate about? Work projects or home projects? Is it over small things or major things?

Once you have insight into your procrastination problem you can find a workable solution. Build on the knowledge you learn about yourself. Start on the project. Even if you make mistakes, they can be corrected. Henry Link once said, "While one person hesitates because he feels inferior, the other is busy making mistakes and becoming superior."

Now take the next step. Develop a prevention program by discovering how to maintain the level of motivation that is best for you, and focus on thinking positively about how to conquer procrastination.

In 1957 a Procrastination Club was formed in Philadelphia. They had several thousand members. They decided to try holding a convention but when the members put off paying their registration, the plans fell apart.

Disorganization

Are supplies, files, and referral materials at your fingertips when you need them? Make a plan and work your plan. Getting organized will take some time but you will discover that it will be well worth it when you can find things easily, do things faster, and know what needs to be done next.

$ $ $ Success Brief $ $ $

Since starting about 20 years ago as a writer and self-publisher of books on parachuting, Dan Poynter and his business, Para Publishing, have blossomed. He not only writes and produces books and is an expert witness on parachuting and hang gliding, but he also has expanded to help others learn how to self-publish. "I have no doubt," says Don, "that my success is due greatly to disciplining myself to be organized."

$ $ $

Spinning Wheels

When you enter your office, do a hundred things that need to be done go through your mind? Do you feel there is so much to do you don't know where to begin? Set your priorities and stick to them. Otherwise, at the end of the day you will realize you only "put out fires" by handling things as they came up. Don't let the spinning wheels syndrome overwhelm you. Decide what is really important to do and then do it. Put the "fires" on hold and go forward by sticking to the plan of the day.

Forgetfulness

Have you ever remembered something that needs to be handled and then forgotten it only to remember it again a few days later and then a week later again? You are wasting precious creativity and thought production because of mind clutter. When you have too much on your mind and can't think straight, you are experiencing clutter overload. Next time you think of something that needs to be done, write it down and free your mind. You will be amazed at how relieved you will feel and how your creative juices begin flowing again.

A time-management expert once said, "A thought committed to paper *frees* the mind." That says it all. If you truly want to see a difference in your time-management skills, the most important thing to do is write things down. Don't assume you will remember later. Free your mind by writing it down right then and there—when you think of it.

MAKE A ROAD MAP TO SUCCESS

This how-to book would be leaving out an important ingredient of making your business work if it didn't address one of the basics. That is, the importance of making a "success" list every single day. This is a method of writing down everything that needs to be done so you have a plan to follow.

Would you ever go on a trip without a road map? No. You would have a focus of where you are going and which route you should take to arrive at your destination. We tend to do more planning for a trip than we do for life. Don't let a day pass you by without charting your road map to success. In essence, this success list is a compilation of short-term goals. It is your focus of what you are going to do. It shows you what route to take to get things done and how you will reach your destination.

Begin by purchasing a week-at-a-glance or a month-at-a-glance calendar. Seeing a month at a time is mind-boggling for most people, but if it works for you, then use it. It doesn't matter if it is a Day Timer, Day Runner, or any other brand. What is imperative is that you get one and use it to help you accomplish more every day.

Here are some helps on what to look for and what not to look for when shopping for the calendar book that is right for you.

What to Buy	**What Not to Buy**
SIZE:	
One *small* enough so that it is easy to carry in your briefcase, pocket, or purse.	Don't get one so large that you would rather leave it in your car or on your desk. The three-ring notebooks look professional but seldom get used. They simply aren't practical.
NAME & ADDRESS SECTION:	
Make sure there is a *name and address section* in your book. This is where you keep doctors, repairmen, and baby-sitters' phone numbers in case there's an emergency and you are away from home.	Don't purchase a separate Name and Address Book. This only gives you more to carry.

PAD OF PAPER:

Look for a datebook with a blank pad of paper included or at least one that has room for a pad. You will need extra paper from time to time.	If you rely on separate sheets of paper then you will have to remember to insert them into the datebook when needed.

As soon as you have purchased the datebook that best fits your needs, start filling in all the important dates you can think of such as project deadlines, doctors appointments, family birthdays, anniversaries, and so on. Write these in red ink to help them stand out from your everyday entries. Your personal, professional, and social life all goes in this *one* calendar. Jot down things as you think of them and enter each item on the day it needs to take place. For instance, if you promise to call someone once a week to get a business report, then write it in your book each week on that day because this frees your mind.

It has been said that a sign of genius is to write things down as you think of them. Some of the world's greatest composers and inventors have had this trait in common. If you tend to be creative at all, you will notice a big difference once you begin writing things down.

When you know you have a big project deadline coming up, jot it down *on the due date.* Jot down little sub-deadlines for completing each component of the task that needs to be done *before* the due date. For instance, if you have a proposal due next month on the fifteenth, write down that the fifteenth is the deadline. But, on the first, write down "Research ABC project at the library." On the fifth, "Make the phone call it will take to get facts needed," and so on.

This works in your personal life, too. When you finish getting a haircut and know you will need another cut in six weeks, note it in your book a week early so you can make the appointment. When you get into your car immediately after dropping off clothes for dry cleaning, make a note of the day you are to pick them up in your datebook.

Be sure you keep track of your personal and professional life in *one book.* Never carry a separate calendar for work, one for home, one for social appointments.

Tip: If a client mentions a special date, like their company's anniversary date or their own birthday, jot it down in your datebook. Mail a card or send flowers and they will think you're wonderful! Many smart business people take the time to get to know their clients. Keep their special event dates in your calendar. This also keeps your business and name forefront in the client's mind, which could mean a sale when the need arises for your product or service.

When will you find the time to fill in datebook activities? It's easy. Fill it in while watching television, standing in lines, waiting for an appointment, over lunch, sitting in traffic, or even when waiting for the kids to come out of school. (Besides, having something to do helps relieve the frustration of sitting and waiting.) You will be amazed at how many times during the day you can grab a few extra seconds to jot something down.

You will soon realize that glancing at your datebook without the items listed in any particular order is discouraging. Because you have been writing things down for weeks as you think of them, the problem is that there is not any organization to the list. For instance, look at tomorrow's date where you may first have listed a phone call, then an appointment, another phone call, a project deadline, and another appointment. Who wants to refer to a disorganized list all day long and have to sort out what does and does not take priority? The solution? Take five minutes the night before to plan and prepare for the next day.

Take a piece of paper from the pad in your datebook and clip it to the front of your datebook. Divide your paper into three sections: *Calls, Go's, Do's.* Under each section fill in what needs to be done by drawing from information that you have listed for the next day inside the datebook. Any phone calls you need to initiate or return go under the *Calls* section on your piece of paper. Any

---

CALLS

Joan—prices
Health Assn.—re endorsements
X *Recording studio—re appt.*
Ron—typeset costs
X *Hair appt.*

GO's

Library—research on lists
X *10:00—Anita appt.—Marketing*
X *1:00—Dr. D—lunch*
Art Shop—get transparencies
Hardware Store—hooks for offc.
X *P.O. box & mail proposals*

DO's

X *write Johnson—samples*
mail contract—lawyers offc.
write thank you's
send Mom copy re vitamins
X *redo script*
X *order folders—press releases*
send Visa payment

appointments or errands are for your *Go's* section. Everything else will go under your *Do's* section. For instance, a *Do* might be balancing the checkbook, looking up a number in the Yellow Pages, or doing the laundry. As you make your list, mark an *X* in front of any areas that are absolute priority for the day. This way, when you glance at the list during the day, you are alerted to the things that positively have to be done. Then, if there is time left over, you can do some of the things that aren't marked with an *X*. But, concentrate on the top priorities before doing anything else.

Now as you journey through your day, you only need to refer to the list on the front of your datebook which is compiled in an orderly manner. As you complete each item or appointment, cross it off. At the end of each day, one glance at your To-Do List tells you how many projects, calls, and errands you handled. Whatever you don't get done transfer to the next day's list.

I love to sit on the edge of the bed at night and check over my list to be sure everything I accomplished is crossed off. My husband has caught me more than once writing in something that wasn't on my original list just so I could cross it off. It's a great feeling of satisfaction. Note the sense of accomplishment you feel. Isn't it wonderful? *Enjoy* crossing things off your list. You deserve it! You will also sleep better because your mind will be free of thinking about everything that needs to be done tomorrow.

Transferring the undone items to the next day also gives you some perspective about how well you are managing your time. If you notice yourself transferring something day after day after day, then you need to stop and analyze *why*. Get it done and over with so you can cross it off.

During my years of speaking and consulting, I have seen many businesses and personal lives turned around by using this method to plan their days. "I can't believe what a difference a simple list can make in how much I get done in one day," said one administrative assistant. Lucy McRae, a real estate executive commented, "I have always used a To-Do List, but it wasn't divided into sections and I dreaded referring to it. This Call, Go, Do method has changed my life." Your datebook will become your best friend. After using it only a few days, you will discover a new freedom and sense of well-being.

DEFINING PAPERWORK PROCEDURES

As you begin developing systems and procedures for your home office, you will notice there are many things you do over and over. Rethinking, creating, and filling in the same letter or form day in and day out takes time away from other things you could be doing. Take a moment to establish routines for this type of repetitive work. This will save you hours in the future and allow you to be more efficient. The mark of a true business professional is responding to all calls and letters within twenty-four hours. Here are some ways to help you get organized and save time concerning paperwork.

Handling Correspondence

One way to handle repetitive correspondence is to develop form letters for quick response. Set up a folder or notebook with several different letters and label them letter A, B, or C. For instance, form letter A might contain information on how the customer can return a damaged product to you; form letter B might express thanks for a customer's order; form C could include some comments about your working on their claim, or thanking the customer for a payment. When you receive correspondence, decide which form letter gives the proper response, and then mark an *A, B,* or *C* in the corner as a sign to you, or your secretary, of which form letter to use. Of course, be sure to always personalize the letter already on the computer by filling in the correct date and the name of the person to whom you are addressing the letter.

Tip: When you have completed correspondence to a person, place a check mark in the corner of his original letter with the date when the answer or action was completed, or attach a copy of your response.

A fast and personal way to respond informally is by using a Post-it with a brief note as a reply. Every piece of correspondence does not require a formal response. If, when opening the mail, you find there is some correspondence that could be handled easily, either write your reply across the bottom of their letter (and keep a copy) or attach a Post-it with your reply and send it back. Do things in the quickest, most efficient way.

How do you decide what to do with paper when it first comes across your desk? Handling paperwork seems never-ending sometimes. But you *can* get control of it if you don't ever handle any piece of paper more than once. That's right! As soon as you read it the first time, put it in its place. This way it's taken care of right then and there.

Have you ever heard of the **"Dot Method"**? It was created by some dear person to whom I would like to give credit, but, I have never found out his or her name. Every time you handle a piece of paper, place a dot in the corner. After a week or so, if you end up with paper that looks like it has the measles, you know you need to adopt better methods of managing paperwork.

The Five-Step Method for Handling Paper. Every day, at least once a day, gather up all the papers on your desk. Quickly sort through everything and place every piece of paper in the appropriate file:

1. Do It Now
2. Low Priority
3. Later Reading
4. File
5. Trash (the "round file")

If you do this each day, you will never again find yourself surrounded by mounds of paperwork.

The **Do It Now** file might be a different color to signify that it is top priority. It is a good idea to keep stand-up files on *top* of your desk for easy access. If they are filed away in a drawer, it often becomes a case of "out of sight and out of mind." There are some colorful stand-up racks and matching folders that look nice enough to leave out on top of the desk.

Sorting mail should be taking only a few minutes. The most important thing to remember is not to read every magazine, brochure, or advertisement that crosses your desk. Put it in a reading file for later if it is something you are interested in at first glance. If there is any question in your mind as to whether you'll want to read it later, throw it away *now*. The junk mail and no-interest mail gets tossed immediately.

As you open and read each letter, write notes in the margin of the *key* points to summarize the letter. Or, an even bigger time-saver is to have a highlighting pen close at hand and highlight the key points. When you are ready to respond with a phone call or letter, these notes or highlighted areas will allow you to take quicker action. You won't need to reread that piece of mail later. If you have a secretary, train her to highlight the key points for you.

Work Order Forms are an excellent method of jotting down what needs to be done for incoming work such as typing or copying. If you have a clerical person working for you, a Work Order Form is a lifesaver when you are out of the office. It helps furnish the proper information such as deadlines, draft or final copy, enclosures, and other specific instructions. If your "staff" consists of you and only you, the Work Order Form saves you from having to rethink what needs to be done. Use it for copying to be done, to note that a letter needs an enclosure, or just to mail something off by a particular date. The Work Order Form will be your reminder.

Work Order Form

NEED BY DATE: _____

TODAY'S DATE: _____

PAPER: Plain   Letterhead

TYPING FORM: MEMO   DRAFT   FINAL

SPACING: Double   Single

COPIES TO: Computer file   Main file

    Other: _____

ENCLOSURES: _____

NEED ENVELOPE?   Regular   Large

SPECIAL INSTRUCTIONS: _____

_____

_____

RETURN WORK TO: _____

                                  (person filling in form)

Type four of these forms to an 8½-by-11 sheet. Copy onto bright-colored paper. Cut them apart and *voila!* These bright forms can be attached to each piece of work and instructions are easily accessible when needed. I have used them successfully for years, from working with nine supervisors to working for myself. They will work wonders for you as well.

How Is Your Office Filing System?

Filing always tends to get put on the back burner as low priority. What happens is that eventually we need a particular letter or document and at that point, when it cannot be found, the filing becomes **top priority.** If your idea of filing is waiting until the "to be filed" pile is five inches thick, change your thinking.

Time experts say that 80 to 90 percent of all files are never referred to again. That is why the "round file" (trash) should be close by. If you just "think" you might need to keep a paper for the future, throw it away rather than have it take up space sitting in the cabinet. Do not be a collector. Space is a real commodity when you work out of your home. As your home-based business grows, you will find there is not a lot of extra storage space available. So, you have to make every inch count by working for you, not against you.

One survey of leading American organizations found that the average executive spends nearly four workweeks a year hunting for misfiled or missing information. Management engineers have put a dollar value on this lost time, saying the cost of a single misfile ranges between $61 and $73.

Pendaflex tells us some of the most common causes of misfiles are:

- **Improper indexing.** Make sure that papers to be filed are clearly identified as to name or subject.
- **Illegible labels.** Folders should be clearly identified, preferably with type-written labels.
- **Inadequate guiding.** The rule of thumb is 15 to 20 guides per drawer.
- **Overloaded folders.** Folders should contain no more than one-half to three-quarters of an inch of paper.
- **Overcrowded file drawers.** Leave four to six inches of space in each drawer for better visibility of tabs and working ease.
- **Lack of charge-out devices.** A charge-out system is necessary for control. Stock-out guides are available for this purpose.

The key to a good filing system is to file on a regular basis and keep your system easy and accessible. Here are some guidelines for your filing success:

1. **Title.** Label your file as you most often think of it, i.e., John Smith/ABC Company. If you can never remember a certain person's last name, then file under their first name.
2. **Cross-reference.** If you need to cross-reference, the right way to do it is to

put in a piece of paper with a note spelling out exactly where the reference is located.

3. **Order.** Inside the file, keep the most recent correspondence on the top (in the front) of the folder.

4. **Staple papers together.** Do not allow paper clips in your file. They will only attach themselves to the wrong papers and cause you grief later on.

5. **Enlarge.** Tape or staple small documents to 8½-by-11-inch paper to keep them from getting lost.

6. **Removing.** Never take papers from a file without having a backup copy. It is best to never remove an original. Make a copy to carry with you instead.

Set up a **File** basket along with your **In** and **Out** baskets for real efficiency. Whether you do your own filing or a secretary handles it, there is a better chance of the papers finding a home if they do not have to endure another "sorting" process.

Tickler files are very effective if you use them properly. A tickler file is to tickle your memory about something that needs to be handled later. It helps you clean off your desk and plan ahead. It helps you remember short- or long-term items and projects for follow-up. To make a good tickler system that works, you need 16 file folders!

> 12—one for each month or an accordion file that already has the months marked.
>
> + <u> 4</u>—for each week in the month. Number these 1, 2, 3, and 4.
>   16

Mark on your To-Do List to check your tickler file every Monday to see what reminders you have in that week's file.

DEALING WITH INTERRUPTIONS

An interruption now and then is naturally going to happen. But, watch out for those exasperating interruptions when they begin playing havoc with the entire day. Too many interruptions daily is a sign of a weak communication system or lack of assertiveness. In order to accomplish enough, there are times when you have to close the door or take the phone off the hook for one hour a day. Employing an answering service to take your messages or purchasing a recorder is the ideal situation.

When Children Interrupt

If children are interrupting your work, figure out ways to help them understand when you need quiet time. A toddler's nap time is a great time to dig in and get a lot done. Try scheduling their reading time to coincide with your quiet time. If the children are older and don't take naps, you might try an idea I heard from one mother. The children knew when she placed a hat on her head that she was on an important phone call and was not to be disturbed.

Learn to Say No

Do you have a hard time saying no? Most people have trouble with this type of interruption. Learn to say no tactfully to requests and invitations rather than overdoing. Say no to people who keep asking you to get involved. Here are three rules to follow that will help:

1. **Be Courteous.** Listen to their request.
2. **Say, "No thanks."** Give reasons to help them understand. Tell them if you are overcommitted or that it isn't what you would enjoy doing. Be honest!
3. **Offer a solution/suggest an alternative.** Maybe you remember someone who has mentioned to you that he would like to get involved. Or possibly you can assist in coming up with a more effective way of handling the request.

You will offend fewer people by being honest about your feelings and your time limits. If you feel relieved after saying no, it is reinforcement that you've done the "right" thing.

Telephone Interruptions

Telephones are easier to control if you have a designated time to *return* and *initiate* calls each day. Get names and numbers together to make calls. List topics of conversation briefly next to the numbers. Set aside a particular time each day to return and initiate calls. When you leave messages with others for callbacks, let them know you will be in between the hours of, say, 2:00 P.M. to 4:00 P.M. for calls. Most people are fairly good about returning your call at the time you say you are available because they don't like playing telephone tag any more than you do. If you get a call at a bad time, don't be afraid to say, "I'm not able to talk right now, but I'll call you back later."

Try using a telephone log sheet to keep track of all your phone messages. This not only eliminates interruptions but also keeps all calls on one list. Take a large pad of paper or a tablet and list any calls that need to be returned. As you return and complete each call, cross it off the list. This gives you a record of who still needs to be called and what the call was about. Here is a format to use as your telephone log:

Person's Name	Company Name	Topic	Phone Number

Excessive phone users may want to consider purchasing a set of earphones to eliminate neck strain, shoulder tension, or headaches. When you are telemarketing, for instance, it is important that you don't hold the phone between your shoulder and chin for long periods of time. Earphones cost about fifty dollars and are well worth the price if you are saving money by not going to the chiropractor. These wonderful inventions also free your hands. If you use your hands while talking you will sound more natural to the caller. When talking on the phone, place a mirror in front of you to be sure you are smiling. When you are, it shows in your voice and makes a better impression.

Do whatever you can to fight against interruptions and remember, once you conquer them you will increase your self-confidence and self-management skills.

SETTING PRIORITIES

Establish priorities and evaluate them often. During a busy day, it is especially necessary to evaluate what you are doing and why. Otherwise, you may be doing a low-priority task when a high-priority one is waiting to be done. There is a great deal of difference between urgent and important. Even though something urgent comes up, it may not be as imperative as finishing the important project. As an ongoing evaluation system, stop whatever you are doing several times a day and ask yourself these three questions:

- *Why am I doing this now?* Is it because there is a deadline? Is it important? Is it because I enjoy doing this rather than the task at hand? Am I wasting time?
- *Is there an easier way?* How else can I get this job done? Is there a shortcut? Could it be done in fewer steps? Would it be smarter to have a secretarial service, a direct mail service, or even a temporary person doing this?
- *How can I eliminate steps?* Should this be delegated to someone else? Should I hire someone to get parts of it done rather than doing it all?

After you have asked yourself these questions, you will have a better grasp of everything you do and why you do it. This evaluation method can be valuable in anything you do anytime of the day or night, from making phone calls or working on a project to painting a house or loading a dishwasher. Answer these questions in the space provided. They will help you improve your method of evaluating your priorities.

What in particular can you improve by using this method in your Work Life? _____

_____

What specifically can you improve by using this method in your Homelife? _____

_____

Now you can begin to enjoy these benefits:

- Using your time more effectively
- Distinguishing more readily between important and urgent matters
- Recognizing the best time to achieve particular results
- Finding improved techniques for doing things

Once you evaluate these questions, you will begin to notice how much time you spend spinning your wheels and how much of the time you are actually digging into priorities. Studies have been done that prove businesses spend 85 percent of their time doing things that bring in 15 percent of the profits. Don't be one of these statistics! Figure out better ways to prioritize.

It is human nature to do what we enjoy doing most, first. It takes true discipline to make yourself do the *worst* first. Use the easy, small tasks that you enjoy doing as a reward for doing those things that you don't like to do. It is a substantial relief to get the harder tasks out of the way first. Then, you feel better about yourself and the finished work. The sense of accomplishment is even greater when you get the dreaded things out of the way so you can cross them off your list.

You must prioritize the various tasks in your daily life. Analyze ways to make your life simpler. Of course, no matter how hard you try to prioritize you will find there are times when you have to be flexible and adjustable. But if your priorities aren't determined first, every day will be disorganized. All you can do is your BEST! Plan ahead by learning as much as possible about events that are coming up. You will manage better by allowing whatever *lead time* is necessary to anticipate the work involved.

Time

Take time to WORK.........It is the price of success
Take time to PLAY ....It is the secret of perpetual youth
Take time to THINK ....It is the source of power
Take time to READ ....It is the foundation of wisdom
Take time to PRAY ....It is the greatest power on earth
Take time to LAUGH ......It is the music of the soul
Take time to LISTEN .....It is the pathway to understanding
Take time to DREAM .....It is hitching your wagon to a star
Take time to LOVE
*   and BE LOVED.............It is the gift of God.*

5

Customer Service

"SUPPOSE WE REFUND YOUR MONEY, SEND
YOU ANOTHER ONE WITHOUT CHARGE, CLOSE
THE STORE, AND HAVE THE MANAGER SHOT—
WOULD THAT BE SATISFACTORY?"

A CUSTOMER'S IMPRESSION of an entire organization or company is usually based on a single transaction with the person who first gives them service. Customer service is dealing with people. Every day you deal with people either in person or over the phone. How your company is perceived is determined by the way you come across, and how well you determine the customer's needs.

Have you ever heard someone say he could never sell anything, much less be a salesperson? Little do we realize that we are all in sales each day of our lives because we are constantly *selling ourselves* to others around us. How well we sell ourselves, our products, or our ideas to others depends on how we deal with people. You can make the difference!

Experts who study future trends say people will be demanding more and more service and quality. Customers who become longtime clients will also demand TLC (tender loving care). To be successful you must develop and master the art of winning and keeping new customers.

$ $ $ Sucess Brief $ $ $

Before starting her own home-based business, Gayle Skelton was a labor and delivery nurse. Whenever she was responsible for preparing and cooking food for any of the organizations she belonged to, the members would rave over the food. This prompted her to begin her own catering business, which has since grown to six regular employees and recently moved into a commercial kitchen space. Her income has doubled every year since she started as A Catered Affaire. Gayle's recipe for continued success is a "commitment to personal attention and a high standard of service."

$ $ $

To provide the best service, you have to know what your customers want and need. If your business had to choose between taking a chance and going with a sure thing, which would you choose? *Ask* customers what their wants and needs are rather than gambling and you *have* a sure thing! Gaining this knowledge is critical to customer service.

Customer Service Checklist

To be sure your customer service is the best it can be, place a check mark in front of the areas that are effective for you now. Those you cannot check need some extra attention. Keep working at evaluating and maintaining your customer service until you are able to check off all areas.

___ 1. I put myself in my customer's shoes when checking my advertising to be sure it is not misleading.

___ 2. I use specific guidelines about how consumer problems can be solved by my company, distributors, or retailers.

___ 3. I have developed systems to answer customer inquiries promptly.

___ 4. All mail is acknowledged within 48 hours.

___ 5. My written and verbal communication with customers shows personal concern for their problems.

___ 6. Each problem is given fair treatment and investigation rather than judged on assumptions.

___ 7. I look at each situation from my customer's point of view in helping to solve it.

___ 8. If I cannot make restitution, I am sincere when explaining to a customer why a claim is unjustified.

___ 9. I keep thorough records as to the cause of complaints and I take action to eliminate the problem.

___ 10. I always follow up complaints or compliments from my customers to be sure they are satisfied, or to say thank you.

___ 11. My company regularly reviews procedures to determine how we can be more responsive and productive to our customers.

It is amazing how rarely businesses ask their customers for feedback. Department stores are a perfect example of an industry that lacks needed feedback. They make finding clothes sizes and/or price tags practically impossible. One garment has a tag in the neck, another on the hemline, another fastened under the arm, and some are not sized at all so customers have to search inside the garment. If we can't find a size then we don't bother to try it on. It replaces the joy of shopping with pure frustration. The time spent searching for sizes or prices could be spent trying on and buying. So, who loses? The customer and the store because the customer is unhappy *and* the store doesn't make the sale.

Why do some stores make it so hard to buy when their reason for being in business is to sell products? Correcting the problem would mean more money flow and happier customers. But, have you ever received a call or suggestion card asking for feedback? Customer opinions are a business's greatest resource, and yet this area is relatively untapped.

Even though your home-based business isn't a department store, the principle is the same. Ask yourself if you are making it difficult for your customers to buy. In his book, *Phone Power*, George Walther says, "the difference between SURVIVING and SOARING in the business world is caring." Get critical information from present clients to show you care and to help you soar rather than only survive. Find out what bugs customers, what they like best, what they like least, what would make it easier for them to order or buy, and what services or items they would like provided. The equation is simple: Good customer service equals more sales. To find out what customers want:

- **Ask** for suggestions and ideas over the phone or in person. Or have them fill out an evaluation or questionnaire by mail. (If you offer a coupon or small gift for completing your form, you will get a better return.)
- **Listen** to what they tell you.
- **Appreciate** them by sending a "thank you for your business" note, giving them special service, or offering a discount when they purchase $500 or more worth of products.

Tip: Keep questionnaires easy and brief so they can be done quickly. Multiple choice answers are best.

In a nutshell, these three ingredients are all it takes to gain a loyal customer for life. This expresses to customers how important they are to you and your business. I heard recently about a small local bank that started a pickup-and-delivery service for their customers. They are bound to be successful because they are reaching out to serve customers and listening to what people want.

Listening Skills

If you remember to treat the customer as you would like to be treated, you'll probably discover that, most of all, you like to be listened to. One of the most important aspects of gaining clients and serving is how well we listen to what customers want and need.

Assess your listening skills by circling the number that best fits your answer.

	Almost always	Usually	Some-times	Seldom	Almost never
1. Do you encourage customers to talk?	5	4	3	2	1
2. Do you listen even if you do not particularly like the person who is talking?	5	4	3	2	1
3. Do you listen to the content, not judge the delivery?	5	4	3	2	1
4. Do you put aside what you are doing when listening?	5	4	3	2	1
5. Do you make eye contact with the customer?	5	4	3	2	1

	Almost always	Usually	Some-times	Seldom	Almost never
6. Do you avoid inter-ruptions and distrac-tions?	5	4	3	2	1
7. Do you keep your mind open?	5	4	3	2	1
8. Do you listen for ideas when the cus-tomer is talking?	5	4	3	2	1
9. Do you ask custom-ers to repeat or clar-ify statements you do not understand?	5	4	3	2	1
10. Do you USE repeti-tion to your advan-tage?	5	4	3	2	1

SCORING: If your score is 35 or more you are a GOOD listener.
If your score is 25–30, you are an AVERAGE listener.
If your score is 20 or below, you need to IMPROVE your skills.

Elaine Thomas, an expert on communication skills says, "Of the three ȘILENT skills'—listening, reading, and writing—listening constitutes 45 percent of an individual's daily communications process. Reading follows with 16 percent; writing, a mere 9 percent. For salespeople, listening probably exceeds 45 percent. Did you know that 30 percent of an average person's day is spent talking? This means we spend a total of 70 to 80 percent of our day in some type of communication."

By listening you can learn what a customer is thinking and feeling about you and your product or service. It's like reading between the lines. But, you have to be silent and concentrate and be receptive to find the opportunity in what the customer is telling you. The four most critical things to remember when listening are:

1. Disregard interruptions and distractions
2. Maintain your attention and interest
3. Concentrate on the person
4. Keep an open mind

Listening is a skill that has to be developed because talking is easier than listening. But, once you master this important part of customer service, the customer will have more respect for you, more trust and confidence. And he will more readily accept what you say.

When Will These Phones Stop Ringing?

David Ortiz

DEVELOP TOP TELEPHONE SKILLS

One of the prerequisites of great customer service is knowing how to deal with the telephone. In a recent office survey, telephones were cited as the number one complaint. In a past position as a customer service department manager, I hated to answer the phones because the chances were great that it would be a complaint or problem. Now that I have my own business, I have a new respect for the phones. If the phones don't ring, I don't work. So, now I *love* getting phone calls. When the ringing phone spells *b-u-s-i-n-e-s-s* for you, personally, it takes on a new meaning. The key to conquering the "telephone trauma" lies in our perception and education of how to handle every type of incoming or outgoing call. Once you feel confident, you will enjoy the telephone.

Thirty percent of communication power is lost over the phone. This means we have to try harder to win the caller over. A get-things-done attitude comes across immediately to the caller as does an I-don't-want-to-be-bothered attitude. Put yourself in their shoes. As a call-in customer, what would *you* want? Your answer will probably be either courtesy, attention, satisfaction, or appreciation. These are the same things customers look for, and are good reasons for measuring your telephone skills.

First, listen to your voice intonation. If every time you answer the phone, the caller asks, "Who?" or, "What company?" you may be talking too fast or with a voice pitch that is hard to understand. If your talking voice is too high you will sound hyper. If it is too low, you will sound like a snail on Valium.

When you must put a caller on hold, tell him why and how long before you will check back with him. Try not to make him hold more than one minute without checking back.

How to Eliminate Telephone Tag

If you and a caller are going back and forth and keep missing each other, eliminate the tag game by leaving a specific message as to *when* you can be reached or setting an appointment to call him back. One business I called handled this situation well by saying on their recorded message, "If you'll tell me the best time to reach you back, then we won't miss each other again."

Body Language

We communicate in three ways: nonverbally (body language), verbally, or by the actual words we speak. The nonverbal or body language accounts for 55 percent of our communication impact. This includes eye contact, hand movements, and how we hold ourselves. Our verbal communication accounts for 38 percent of our communication impact. This is expressed by the volume and pitch of our voices and how fast or slow we talk. The actual words we speak account for only 7 percent of our communication impact.

Even over the phone, as impossible as it may seem, callers can hear your body language. For example, when a person is slumped over in a chair, tired, or not feeling well, it is interpreted as inattention. Be sure to sit up straight, unfold your arms, uncross your legs, and smile. Even over the phone, a smile on your face and in your voice comes across quickly in a greeting or conversation.

Understanding body language can help you make a sale and know how to handle a client. When words and body signals do not match, the nonverbal signs are the most reliable. The experts say this is because the body signals come from the subconscious. Here are some signals you will want to know and what action you can take for each situation:

Face Tension . . . When you notice tension on a client's face, it means that he has other things on his mind.

What you can do about it: Try asking more questions about his needs so you can get his attention or discover the problem.

Arms folded over chest . . . When a client stands or sits with his arms folded over the chest, it is a sign that he is totally turned off. (When arms are folded *and* the hands make a fist, the client is angry.)

What you can do about it: Do whatever you can to break this position and you will have a better chance of selling your product or service. You might try handing the client a business card, a brochure, or a pencil to change this "closed minded" posture. (If he is angry, gently ask why.)

Leaning toward you . . . When a person leans toward you, it is a sign that he is very interested and probably already sold on whatever you are saying.

What you can do about it: At this point, you will want to be brief and answer any questions before you close the sale.

Chin stroking . . . This means the client is giving a lot of thought to your offer or proposal.

What you can do about it: Sway him toward your product or service by talking a little more, then be silent and let him decide. (When he stops stroking his chin, he has made up his mind.)

Head down . . . When a person has his head down, it means he is feeling guilty about something.

What you can do about it: He may have decided *not* to buy and he feels guilty about not being able to say no. Give him the opportunity to go home and think about it to let him off the hook.

How Many Rings?

Did you know that answering a ringing phone on the first or second ring affects the caller's view of your company? Tom Peters cites an incident of calling Federal Express 27 times. He noted that 26 of those times the phone was picked up on the first ring. Imagine how important a customer feels when his call is answered quickly. Anytime you can pick up the phone promptly, it displays a "caring" attitude to the customer.

Think about it, have you ever called a place of business where the phone rang and rang before someone answered. What were your feelings? Probably, you wondered if the office was on a coffee break, if they even opened the office that day, or if they just didn't answer because they didn't want to be bothered.

Telephone skills are more powerful than we can imagine. Handle callers with the courtesy you would like to be handled with and notice what a difference it makes.

Phone Skills Checklist

	Often	Sometimes	Rarely
1. I attempt to answer the telephone before the second ring.			
2. I identify myself and the company when answering.			
3. I use body posture that keeps me alert.			
4. I use the caller's name as much as possible during a conversation.			
5. I help eliminate telephone tag by leaving specific messages.			
6. I scan pertinent information before initiating an outgoing call.			
7. I have necessary paper and pens within reach of the telephone.			
8. I apologize sincerely when customers are inconvenienced.			
9. I feel comfortable when dealing with angry customers.			
10. I prioritize my return calls.			

Total up your score by giving yourself:

    10 points for each OFFEN
     6 points for each SOMETIMES
     2 points for each RARELY

Perfect score = 100

HOW TO MAKE A POSITIVE FIRST IMPRESSION

Over the Telephone

The first impression over the phone is formed within ten seconds. This means whether you, a secretary, or an answering machine make the initial contact, it needs to be the best it can be. The proper way to answer a call is:

- Greet the caller—"Good morning."
- State the company name—"ABC Company."
- Identify yourself—"This is Judy."
- Ask how you can help—"How may I help you?"

Watch your voice inflection as you answer. You can come across as either dull or enthusiastic, depending on how you use your voice. Even if you are having a bad day, the greeting *must* be enthusiastic and sound as though you have been anticipating the call.

The next time you call a business, check the impression you get in the first ten seconds. If you employ a person or service to answer your phone, place a call to your own company sometime when you are out of the office, and notice how you are treated. Ask clients and friends for their reaction when they call your company. Be in the know as to what kind of image your telephone etiquette presents to the outside world.

Tip: Have a business friend call your office and you call his office. This way your employees won't recognize your voice and be on their best behavior. Trading information gives you a new perspective.

In Person

It is amazing how few people really know how to shake hands to win customers. Always use a firm handshake when meeting or greeting anyone. Whether we realize it or not, we are quickly judged by our handshake. Think about "wimpy" handshakes you have encountered and how fast you formed your opinion about those people. Your handshake must be firm and friendly to exude confidence. You have ten seconds to win or lose a customer by that all important first impression which usually consists of some type of greeting.

Put a firm handshake together with a smile and look the person straight in the eye as you introduce yourself. This kind of impression gives you an advantage. See yourself through a customer's eyes. How we come across and respond to customers reflects upon us individually and on our company. Find out how you are doing by answering the following questions.

How Do You Respond to Customers?

This form can assist you in seeing yourself through a customer's eyes. How we come across and respond to customers reflects upon us as an individual and on our company. Find out how you "measure up" by answering these questions:

1. Do I greet customers positively? _____
2. Do I make customers feel comfortable and at ease? _____
3. Do I respond to questions in a knowledgeable manner? _____
4. Do I give them my undivided attention? _____
5. Do I make customers feel unique or like a number? _____
6. Do I feel rushed during conversations with customers? _____
7. Am I unsure of myself and my job or really confident? _____
8. When I can't provide certain information the customers require, do I show frustration? _____
9. Is my enthusiasm warm and genuine? _____
10. Does my appearance match my job role? _____
11. Do I talk about customers in front of other customers? _____
12. Do I address customers by their name and title? _____
13. Do I reassure customers by telling them about our superior products and services? _____
14. Do I say and do things that cause the customer to form a good impression about the company? _____

WIN AND KEEP CUSTOMERS

Part of winning and keeping customers is admitting when you are wrong. It's easier to say, "I'm sorry," or, "I goofed," when you are wrong rather than taking a chance on losing a customer. A print shop owner shared a customer service incident that happened to him. One cold, wintry day when the streets were covered in snow and slippery ice, his wife called him at the shop to ask him to stop at the store on his way home to pick up some breadsticks. Considering the bad weather and that the store would be out of his way, he decided to call ahead to be sure they had the breadsticks. The lady who answered the phone in the bakery section assured him they had plenty. He asked her if she would check and hold some for him. He offered his name so she could put them aside, but again she assured him there was not a problem.

He drove out of his way through the ice and snow to reach the store. But, when he walked into the bakery section he didn't see a single package of breadsticks on the shelf. A little concerned, he asked the girl behind the counter if she had put them aside for him after all. The girl said she knew nothing about

any breadsticks; she had just started her shift. There was no apology or attempt from her to make the situation right. Becoming more and more infuriated, he left. When he got home he decided to call the store manager and tell him about the incident. The manager expressed no interest and did not offer an apology or explanation.

At this point, the printer vowed to never set foot in that grocery store again. (He had shopped there for many years.) That night at dinner he told his sons and their wives who also bought their groceries at the same store. After he shared this incident with them, they also decided to shop elsewhere. Losing three customers over a 59-cent package of breadsticks is an example of poor customer service. Translated into dollars, every customer is worth $50,000 to a grocer. And yet, it happens every day. Caring ... service ... showing the customer we want their business by going the extra mile is the way to win and keep customers. It is said that every *unhappy* customer tells ten other people.

For two years now, Raquel Nipp, owner of a maid service, has excelled in giving great customer service. "Doing something extra for the customer is what makes us different. People remember you when you give good service and do a little more than you have to," she says. Raquel employs five people and has a very successful business. "I ask my customers what they like and don't like. I want to know when something is wrong as much as when it is right. It's the only way to good customer relations and a successful business."

$ $ $

The secret, therefore, is in opening the door of communication and allowing, even encouraging, customers to complain to you. If you don't invite complaints, you have no way of knowing *why* you are losing customers. There is no way of correcting a situation you don't know exists. A customer will complain if he is frustrated, disappointed, angry, or feels let down. Wouldn't you rather have unhappy customers tell you their complaints instead of telling ten other existing or potential customers?

If you have ever wondered what actually happens to customers who *stop* calling, here are the statistics:

WHY CUSTOMERS *STOP* CALLING . . .

1%	Die
3%	Move
5%	Go Other Places
9%	Pricing Reasons
14%	Product Dissatisfaction
68%	Attitude of Indifference from People Handling Them

After studying these percentages, it is easy to see why it is important to make complaining easy. Customers need to air their frustration, disappointment, or anger. When they do not complain it's because they don't feel it is worth the effort or they do not believe the company will do anything about the complaint anyway. Analyze ways in which your business can improve service and *gain* customers.

Dealing With an Angry Customer

Use the four *R*'s to help when you are confronted by an angry customer:

1. Ready yourself by being in control.
2. Reason and listen.
3. Repeat their problem to confirm details.
4. Resolve to settle.

Whether the customer is there in person or on the phone, let him blow off steam and then disarm the anger with an immediate apology. Never allow the customer's anger to escalate yours. Shouting at each other won't accomplish a thing. Instead, speak softly and stay in control. Give the client your complete attention. Taking notes as he speaks is very important to future follow-up and as a record of the complaint. Here is a form to use for handling complaints that simplifies record keeping:

Complaint Work Form

Date: _____

Person Calling: _____   Phone number: ( ) _____

Company: _____   Address: _____

1. READY YOURSELF
   Get ready, keep a logical mind, stay in control.
2. REASON and LISTEN
   Empathize, acknowledge, and apologize.
3. REPEAT PROBLEM BACK TO CALLER
   Take notes, ask questions, understand complaint.
4. RESOLVE
   Ask: How would you like this to be settled?
   Assure them you will research the matter.

How will you acknowledge and follow up on the complaint?
by letter? phone call? telegram? _____
_____

When will you follow up (date): _____
_____

What do you see as the cause of this problem? _____
_____
_____

How can you prevent this complaint happening again? _____
_____
_____

Explain *how* and *when* the final outcome of this complaint was settled:
_____
_____

FIVE STEPS TO COLLECTION-CALLING SUCCESS

Before you fly off the handle about overdue bills, try some simple methods to get clients' attention. There is a possibility they haven't been ignoring you on purpose. They may have forgotten or lost the invoice.

I remember once when someone called me and got nasty and obnoxious about a bill I had just plain forgotten to pay. Rather than send me a reminder, he called, ranting and raving about "people like you who don't pay their debts. . . ." I was embarrassed and angry at the same time, until he finally let me explain that I had not intentionally ignored his invoice but honestly had forgotten to send a check. Of course, then, he was embarrassed about the way he had acted. People turn into monsters when they expect, but don't get, their money.

How much nicer it would have been for him to send me a reminder postcard saying something like, "Oops!—I'll bet you forgot to pay your invoice." That would have been enough. It is always best to give the customer the benefit of the doubt. Many times there are extenuating circumstances as to why a person doesn't pay, such as, a death in the family, an accident, a long trip, or an operation. So, take the "reminder" approach a time or two before taking the collection-call route.

Every business has the unpleasant task of having to make collection calls at one time or another. Do you dread placing the call? Are you properly prepared? Is there an easier way? How can you be in control? If these are some of the questions that have bothered you when trying to collect on an invoice, then these five steps to collection-call success will help.

Spending a few minutes before making the collection call may save you not only time, but also embarrassment. Here are some specifics that will give you good results:

1. **Do your homework**

   a. Get the facts by checking previous calls and notes of past conversations.
   b. Ask any salespeople who may be involved for input and an update on the client's situation.

2. **Check your records**

   a. Has this been a recurring problem or is it the first time?
   b. Be sure the customer has been billed previously.
   c. How many reminders have you sent them?
   d. Most important, *check today's mail* in case payment just arrived.
   e. Is there any customer problem that needs follow-up which may be the reason they have not paid the bill?

3. **Find the right person to talk to**

   a. Be sure you are asking to speak to the "right" accounts payable person.
   b. Check with their receptionist for the proper contact person's name and the best time to reach him.

4. **The bottom line**

   a. Do you need full payment or can you negotiate for partial payment, if necessary?

   b. How are you going to handle any objections, indifferences, or anger?

5. Make your action plan

   a. Write out a script of what you are going to say with particular points or
      questions you need to ask.

   Knowing the status of each particular case will give you the ammunition
needed to build a tactful, yet firm foundation for taking action. Now you are
totally prepared and knowledgeable before you make the call. When you know
all the answers to any questions or arguments they might raise, you are in
control and have the leverage to respond. Being able to respond quickly results
in building more self-confidence for you and a customer with a better attitude
who is more willing to pay.

   Who knows? You may even get so good at handling collection calls, you
will learn to like doing it. When you see past due money rolling in, you'll know
you have learned the secret.

6.
Managing Your Stress

WITH TOO MUCH STRESS you will be easily overwhelmed, irritable, overly tired, and have a tendency toward illness. On the other hand, if you have too little stress you will be bored, frustrated, unhappy, and also have a tendency toward illness. When you find the right amount of stress in your life you will have more productivity, creativity, motivation, and good health. Stress is the glue that holds us together.

What is stress? Webster defines stress as "any adjustment to change." Stress isn't the change itself, it is how we perceive and react to the change when it occurs. By learning to handle the inevitable changes that happen each day, we can better control our stress. Changes *are* going to occur daily. When we realize we have to face and attack the change rather than ignoring or withdrawing from it, then we have the upper hand. Believe me, if you don't learn to control stress, it will control you. Harris and Associates conducted a poll of 1,256 adults across the nation which determined that 89 percent of all adult Americans report experiencing high stress; 59 percent said they feel "great stress" at least once or twice a week, and 30 percent report living with high stress nearly every day. Even though there is a great deal of stress produced by working for someone else, you have even more pressure as a home-business manager, because your livelihood depends on only you. This creates further tension and a greater expectation of what you have to accomplish each day.

What are the symptoms of stress you experience day in and day out? Here are the most common signs:

- Headaches
- Exhaustion
- Short temper/Anger
- Frustration
- Stomachaches
- Tight muscles
- Irritability
- High shoulders

In the beginning stages, these stress indicators do not seem too serious, but in more advanced stages, they develop into major problems. Stress affects us physically and psychologically. It is impossible to have emotional (or psychological) stress without our physical bodies also being affected.

In the United States today, 85 percent of all hospital beds are filled with patients suffering from stress-related diseases like cancer, heart attacks, strokes, high blood pressure, stomach disorders, and so on. It is a proven fact that now, more than ever before, stress causes most of our minor and major health problems. When you are constantly under high levels of stress, a breakdown is going to occur, either mental or physical.

UNDERSTAND AND COPE WITH EVERYDAY PRESSURES

It's important to understand what stress is and what makes your life stressful. Anytime you are under tremendous stress, think back and focus on figuring out what really caused you to reach this state. This may help you to avoid it next time. Until you admit there is a problem, you cannot correct it. Get in touch with what causes you stress. Is it things like this:

- Standing in line
- Losing a bill that needs to be paid
- Your in-laws visiting
- Playing telephone tag

- Waiting for a slow elevator
- Misplacing your car keys
- A burned-out light bulb
- Being stuck in traffic

Take the following exercise by writing down **What** causes stress for you. Whether it is a family situation, always running late, or not being able to find things, be sure you put it on the list. Under the **How** column write down ways you can effectively deal with this stress. For instance, if a family situation is the cause, decide you will confront the person and settle the problem. If the stress comes from always running late, commit to getting up a little earlier or preparing the night before to save the morning stress. Take a moment to put things in their place so you won't lose them. The point is to stop and think about how you can eliminate the stressful situations in your life. Write down everything you can think of, and then add to the list as other stressors occur so you can actually *plan* a way to deal with each one.

WHAT CAUSES STRESS   HOW I CAN DEAL WITH IT
_____   _____
_____   _____
_____   _____
_____   _____
_____   _____
_____   _____
_____   _____

Good Time Management Reduces Stress

In the previous chapter, we discussed why it is important to set priorities and plan each day. It is impossible to be a good stress manager without also having good time-management skills. They go hand in hand. A person who manages his time well will have much less stress than someone who does not handle time well. The very act of disorganization will *cause* stress.

Ten years ago Peggy Zadina moved her business as a commercial interior designer into a room attached to the garage. "I learned to juggle everything from field work, drafting, and office work to home responsibilities, and being a wife and mother," she says. "I have to be extremely disciplined and organized with good time-management skills. Setting priorities is the only way." She chose having her own business over a 9-to-5 job for "schedule flexibility, spending more time with my children, freedom, and less stress."

$ $ $

There are two kinds of stress, positive and negative. For example, the positive stress might come from anticipating a meeting with a company that wants to order additional product, from walking down the aisle to take marriage vows, or from the feeling you get in a competitive game when the score is tied. These set off adrenaline in your system that is almost like a high. But the negative stress, like you experience sitting in bumper-to-bumper traffic, running late for an appointment, or hearing from a client who cancels a contract is the kind of stress that you have to watch out for.

Each time a change occurs in your life, remember: It isn't the change itself that causes stress; it's how you perceive and react to the change. Your reaction is based on your perception *of* the change and your attitude *toward* the change.

YOU HAVE A CHOICE

In every situation you have a choice of reacting positively or negatively. Always choose to find another method of handling these negative kinds of stress before frustration or anger sets in. Let's take these same stressful situations from above and use them as examples of the kind of choices we have and how they could be handled.

Situation	Negative Reaction	Positive Reaction
Sitting in bumper-to-bumper traffic	Let it ruin your day by getting you uptight and tense.	Listen to the radio to relax, or improve your mind with an educational tape.
Running late for an appointment.	Arrive upset, late, and frazzled.	Realize you have no control over the traffic. Stop and call your appointment to explain so you won't have to rush.

A client cancels his service contract with you.	Sound angry and bitter, losing any chance of his doing future business.	Put energies into finding out *why* you lost the contract and *what* you can do so it doesn't happen again. Then perpetuate new clients.

_____

_____

_____

_____

_____

In the blank spaces, add to this list any situations you encounter frequently. Then list ways to react differently (more positively) than you usually do. Don't wait for things to happen, make them happen in a way that is best for you. Choose to steer your life in the direction of lower stress.

Have you ever been a passenger in a car with someone who gets all upset over driving behind a "slow" car? Even though the other lanes are all clear, the driver complains about the "slow guy in front" of him while anger escalates. Remember, there is always a choice. Rather than getting steamed at the situation, he can choose to move to another lane. Most times controlling stress is as simple as making a choice. Do you stay here in this lane and get frustrated or is there another way and you only need to make the choice?

Too Many Newscasts

Be aware that listening or watching news programs to start and end your day can have a negative effect on you. Notice how often you listen to the news throughout a day. It's always "bad" news. You can choose to start and end your day on a more positive or upbeat note by listening to music, watching an inspirational show, or reading your Bible. When you are listening only to negative news, whether locally or from all over the world, you can't help feeling down. See how much better your day goes when you choose to listen to something else other than news. Try it for a week and you'll notice a big difference.

In looking back over your biggest hurdles in life, you usually discover that whenever things went wrong there was always a good reason. Don't forget, God has a plan for you. If you look to Him for guidance, things always turn out better. Can you recall something that, when it happened, seemed impossible to accept, but now you say, "Boy, if that hadn't happened as it did, things would not have turned out so well." I often wonder if He gives us the hindsight to capture a "glimpse" of that special plan He has for each of us.

Once you realize that you have a choice, you can turn the negative stress into a positive. But when you allow the change to get the best of you, the situation itself gives you stress. Too many of us do not control the stress by taking advantage of the choices. Here's a humorous slant to a bad day:

You Know It's Going to Be a Bad Day When . . .

You call Suicide Prevention and they put you on HOLD.
Your blind date turns out to be your ex-wife.
You put your bra on backwards and it fits better.
You see a "60 Minutes" news team waiting in your office.
Your birthday cake collapses from the weight of the candles.
Your car horn sticks accidentally as you follow a group of Hell's Angels
*   on the freeway.*
You walk around the block and find your dress is stuck in the back of
*   your pantyhose.*
Your income tax check bounces.
Your wife says, "Good morning, Bill," and your name is George.

When our bodies cannot handle any more negatives, breakdown occurs causing health problems. I found this out the hard way, from the personal experience of enduring a stress disorder called TMJ (Temporo mandibular joint dysfunction, referring to the joint in front of the ears). After clenching my teeth together for years and listening to popping and clicking in my jaws, pain developed and began to grow worse and worse. Before I knew it, I had excruciating headache, ear, and neck pain. Nine doctors and thousands of dollars later, I realized that they kept telling me this was a stress disease. After being in constant 24-hour-a-day pain for three years, I was finally able to control my stress and the pain. It took me a year to research, study, and conquer TMJ. I chose to take charge of my life and you can too, by recognizing and handling stress when you first realize it is getting the best of you. Here are some of the things I learned in order to change my life-style and cope with stress. They will help anyone under stress.

17 WAYS TO REDUCE JOB AND PERSONAL STRESS

1. Incorporate something you love to do into your daily life by finding a balance between work and play. For example, if you love music, set aside some time to play an instrument or sing every day, even if it is only for 30 minutes. If you love to play tennis, find the time and decide you are a priority. It will serve as relaxation.

2. Check your attitude. Think positively about yourself, your day, and the work that needs doing.

3. Delegate effectively. Take inventory of your typical day's work and notice whether there are things you *could* have delegated to someone else (a secretarial service, a fast-copy printer, a high school student to collate, etc.).

4. Take your lunch and breaks. Recharge your batteries by getting away physically and mentally from the work. Take a brisk walk around the block, read the newspaper, anything you like, as long as it isn't work.

5. Learn to relax each day. Close your door, put your feet up for five minutes, and take your mind off the problems of the day.

6. Break down big projects into smaller, easier-to-handle segments. Use the 22-minute rule: When you have a huge project staring you in the face, instead of looking at it as a task that is overwhelming, set a timer for 22 minutes. It will surprise you to see how much you can get done before the timer sounds. You will see progress and realize the importance of breaking a project down to get it done. It helps you put a job into perspective. For example, we are living in such a weight-conscious age, if you had to lose 20 pounds, you would look at the task as losing only 1 pound at a time. Twenty pounds would seem too overwhelming to think about, so you look at it as needing to lose 1 pound. After you lose that pound, you work on losing the next pound. So it is with your work. Don't bite off more than you can chew. Set a timer and break it down. It works!

7. Eat sensibly. Eating, sleeping, and exercising sensibly are vital to controlling stress. If you are doing only two correctly and leaving out the third, it will make a difference in how your system copes. Be sure you are eating the proper foods every day. Watch out for saturated fats and increase fruits, vegetables, and grains.

There is a definite relationship between the food and drinks we ingest and how we feel. Some foods are known for producing energy, sluggishness, positive attitude, or irritability. Pay attention to how you feel physically and mentally after eating certain foods.

Experiment with foods at different times throughout the day. Try eating a big meal for breakfast and a very light lunch. Or, perhaps you feel better when you don't eat any big meals at all and eat several small ones instead. The same way that some people need more or less sleep than others, you may need more or less food than someone else or completely different foods than another.

8. Sleep properly. Your sleep requirements may be different than someone else's, but find out how many hours you need to be at your best. Then, be sure you get that amount of sleep daily.

9. Exercise regularly. Did you know it is a proven fact that people who exercise regularly are more creative, less tense, and emotionally more stable? Even when you don't feel like it, at least do some kind of light exercise every day. Take a brisk walk around the block. Gradually increase a 5-minute walk to 20 minutes, then 30 minutes.

If your job requires you to sit at a desk most of the day, there are some exercises you can do at your desk that will not only make you feel better but also reduce stress.

For the shoulders and neck: Let your head hang forward touching your chin to your chest. Slowly roll your head to the right while breathing in. Repeat to the left. Let your head swing like a pendulum from side to side. Exhale when you roll to the front.

While inhaling, lift both shoulders toward your ears. Then slowly drop them back to normal position while exhaling.

Shoulders and back: Stretch your arms reaching toward the ceiling as far as you can. Inhale as you look up. As you lower your arms back to the normal position, exhale.

Lower back: Sitting up straight with both feet flat on the floor, drop your head to your chest. Inhale as you slowly drop your upper body toward your knees. Exhale and relax. As you inhale, keep the head down and start rolling back up to starting position.

Legs and feet: Take one foot at a time, hold it up off the floor out in front of you. Make a circle, then reverse direction. Repeat with the other leg.

These exercises will help you get the circulation going when you have been sitting too long. Exercise gives you a new lease on life, but you must do it regularly.

When depression visits: Watch out because depression breeds inactivity. The more depressed you are, the more you tend to want to sit and do nothing which causes more depression. Get up and make yourself move around. As soon as you do, you will begin to feel better. Even if you can only make it outside to do a few knee bends and inhale deeply, you will immediately begin to feel better and depression will lift.

Watch your posture when you are feeling depressed. If you stand up straight you will automatically begin to feel better. Play some upbeat music to pick up your spirits or call a friend who is always upbeat.

10. Have fun! Do things for the sheer enjoyment of it. How many times a day do you do something *just for you?* Every day you probably do things for a spouse, a friend, a child, or a neighbor. But, how often do you do something just for you? Over half of us don't do anything for ourselves on a daily basis. Be sure you grab all the gusto you can get in life. Don't take life so seriously. It is already serious enough being bogged down with responsibilities. Give yourself 45 seconds and write down all the fun things you can think of that you either do now for yourself or that you would like to do. Then make a point of doing at least one of them each day. At first, you may have to *learn* to have fun. If so, that's okay. Just be sure to learn it well because your happiness, balance, and success in life depend on how confident and at ease you are with yourself. To believe in yourself and be your best, you must love yourself enough to schedule time for *you*. If you need to, schedule yourself on your To-Do List. Why not? You schedule everyone and everything else including appointments, calls, picking up the kids after school, projects, and on and on. If you've been saying for a while that you wish you had time to start reading the novel that is sitting on your bookshelf, or start that jogging program, decide you are going to schedule the time. You might write down that you are going to jog at 6:30 A.M. This way you commit yourself to doing it. If you would like to take a bubble bath, schedule it at 9:00 P.M. tonight by writing it on that list. Then, you'll do it! Take some time to control your stress by doing some things just for fun, just for you.

11. Do something unexpected for someone. Plan a surprise for someone. This relieves their stress and yours. Have you ever done something spontaneous for a person and noticed that when you were in the act of doing it your stress and theirs was reduced? It's because you lost yourself. Many times forgetting about our own problems by doing something for someone else helps us feel better about ourselves too. Do something silly. Give someone a flower or a card for no reason. Take someone on a picnic in the middle of winter. They'll never forget it, or you!

12. Analyze ways to simplify life. Find easier ways to do things instead of letting them cause you stress.

a. Buy more clothes so you don't have to do laundry so often.
b. Hire a yard worker to mow the lawn now and then to give yourself a break.
c. Use the dry cleaners more instead of washing clothes by hand.
d. Take mending to a seamstress rather than letting it pile up and never getting to it.
e. Shop by catalog to save the stress of traffic, finding a parking place, searching for the right size or color, and standing in line to pay.
f. If balancing your checkbook is a stressor to you, hire an accountant to do it.

Once you consider how much stress you'll save by finding ways to make your life simpler, you will be amazed how you immediately lower your stress level.

13. Improve yourself intellectually by taking a self-improvement course, buying a how-to cassette, or reading regularly.

14. Settle an argument or disagreement with a friend or family member. Confronting instead of ignoring the situation will ease stress.

15. Don't overdo being competitive. Trying to top others can be very stressful. Know when to quit and enjoy competition.

16. Find a friend you can trust and talk to. Don't cut yourself off from others.

17. Repair broken things. The things that are frustrating to you need your attention. One of the biggest stressors to most people is things that need to be fixed. If you are putting up with a watch that has a broken band, a faucet that doesn't work right, or even a button that needs to be sewn on, you are placing a lot of stress on yourself. If you have ever had a taillight out and just keep meaning to get it repaired, but you never quite get around to it, you know what I mean. And yet, it keeps on nagging at you. Make a point to get things repaired and working. Set a goal to call the plumber one month, take clothes to a seamstress the next, and get the car repaired the following. This is the only way to stop that kind of stress.

Listen sometime to what others tell you causes stress for them. It's always the little things in iife that get us down. When she leaves the lid off the toothpaste every morning, it makes you furious. When he kicks his shoes off when walking through the door, she bristles. When a person is preoccupied watching TV and not listening to you talk, you can hardly keep from kicking the television screen. It's not the major move or switching jobs that causes the most stress, it's the little things. Once you learn to take it all in stride and not let a situation become upsetting, you have found a way to cope with life's stressors.

Treat Yourself Well

Psalm 23 calls us to stillness, quiet, rest, and devotion time. We can all know the peace that passes all understanding if we are quiet, relaxed, and listen on a daily basis. Be sure that you give your mind and body a chance to unwind and heal itself regularly. You can't burn the candle at both ends. Your body won't stand for such abuse. It must be treated well each and every day. Stop and rest, take a good break, ride a bicycle, get a massage—just do *something* as a break from work, work, work. If you relax regularly, it will make a difference in your outlook and your productivity.

You have to take care of yourself. No one can follow you around each day to keep reminding you to eat right, sleep enough, exercise, and rest properly. When you realize this, you will begin to see that as much as loved ones care for us, they cannot make us take care of ourselves. We have to monitor our own wellness.

Take a Tranquilizer

There are three natural tranquilizers in life. And guess what? They don't cost a dime. They don't require any prescription. They don't have any negative side effects and will enable you to lead a fuller, more productive life. Use them often and learn how to incorporate them into your life!

Music
- Play soft, relaxing music when you are working
- Play cassette tapes in your car or just sit quietly and listen to your favorite music after a busy day
- Sing or play an instrument

Laughter
- Read a joke book
- Find something funny in everything
- Laugh more at yourself and at life
- Rent a video that is lighthearted and funny

Exercise
- Schedule time on your To-Do List to exercise daily
- Take a brisk walk around the block every day
- Join a health club
- Buy an exercise video

ATTENTION: WORKAHOLICS

If you are a workaholic, you are cheating yourself out of living a full life. You are also a candidate for the Coronary Club. Here are the requirements:

Coronary Club Membership Requirements

- *Continue working each evening instead of spending time to relax, be with a friend or a spouse.*
- *Never say "NO" to a request or an invitation.*
- *Avoid eating restful, relaxing meals. Instead, plan a meeting for every meal.*
- *DO NOT waste time having fun. Avoid sheer enjoyment.*
- *Work through holidays and weekends. Avoid taking any days off.*
- *NEVER delegate responsibility to anyone else. Carry the whole load yourself.*
- *Review all the troubles and worries of the day.*
- *NEVER worship, pray, or meditate. And, if you MUST do these things, be sure to keep one eye on the clock.*

If you are doing any or all of these things now, then you are a workaholic. It takes great discipline to change a workaholic habit, but, you must change your life-style to survive. First, admit you are a workaholic. Here are some problems most workaholics experience and some suggested solutions:

1. Are you a perfectionist? Many workaholics are. Wanting to do your absolute best on every project is commendable. However, to live a balanced, full life, you can't work all the time.

2. Are you making time for yourself and others? Give yourself a break.

3. Are your self-expectations too great? Don't allow yourself to have unrealistic expectations. Be sensible. If the problem is too much work for one person, it can be solved easily by hiring either a temporary or permanent person to relieve the load.

4. Are you skipping lunch or eating while working? This is "normal behavior" for a workaholic. Those around you will notice you are overworked and grouchy because about midafternoon you will probably have hunger pangs or indigestion and be miserable.

When to Stop

When you start making mistakes or misplacing things, it is time to quit for a while. Stop what your are doing and do something else before frustration sets in. At this point, you just need a change of pace. Take a break and come back later to start fresh. Know when to quit!

A great way for a workaholic to begin the healing process is to get away from your work at a specific time each day. Leave work at work and home at home. When you are working out of your home, concentrate on giving your all

DON'T Dump Your Work Problems at Home

where you are—at home or at work. But leave work problems behind a closed office door, just as you leave your personal problems behind when entering your office in the morning. Then, put work aside in the evenings to return to your personal life.

Your stress will be high and constant if, when you leave your office, you dump all your problems on your spouse or a friend. When you talk about it all evening, you don't really get away from it physically or mentally. Talking about it has the same effect as doing it. You might as well have stayed in the office working.

When you discover the discipline you need to separate home and work, self-esteem will increase. There *is* more to life than work, work, work!

Separate Home and Work

Whether you are working on job tasks or home tasks, be sure you are concentrating on the work at hand. One of the greatest challenges you will face will be combining home and office duties. Because you will probably not be used to working at home when you first start your business, you will notice that all kinds of duties that "need to be done" crop up in your mind. You will think of yardwork, repairs, or cleaning and washing that you could be doing while you work.

It's important to work regular hours, whether the best schedule for you is 9:00 A.M. to 5:00 or 3:00 P.M. to 11:00. Work the same number of hours as regularly as possible. Do the lawn work or the wash at the same time you did before you started your home office. Otherwise, before you know it, the day will pass you by and you'll discover you're only accomplishing things around the house instead of office work.

$ $ $ Success Brief $ $ $

Growing tired of the corporate world, Jan Dean, couldn't stop dreaming of having her own business someday. She began by building her consulting business part-time until it grew enough for her to leave her position at General Dynamics as a Small Business Officer. Now she is in demand as a consultant and workshop leader for other home-based business conferences. Jan Dean Associates is a very successful company and highly respected by other home businesses. When asked what she likes best about having her own business, she answered, "The freedom to look out windows when working. My previous corporate office didn't have any windows. And it's fun doing what I love most and keeping irregular hours. Many times I work 1:00 P.M. to 10:00 instead of 9 to 5. It's wonderful to work when I want to."

$ $ $

Workaholics, if you have a hard time stopping to relax periodically and won't pause now and then to sit with your feet up during a lunch break, then

**Keep Homelife and
Office Life Separate**

play with the dog instead. A walk around the block after eating not only helps you forget about work, it is also good for digestion. Don't allow yourself to start doing little projects or you will not want to stop and get back to office work. It's like trying to eat one potato chip or one cookie. Once you start, you can't stop at only one! Always get the harder, most dreaded projects out of the way first. Then, the little tasks are a piece of cake.

7

For People With a Home-Based Business

WHETHER YOU ARE A WOMAN OR A MAN, single or married, with your own home office, you need to streamline and find ways to make your domestic life easier. When working at home, other duties like keeping up with the dishes, yard, laundry, home maintenance, cleaning, groceries, and the children are a big part of entrepreneurism. Just about the time your ego begins to glow as you see yourself becoming a sought-after expert in your field, something goes wrong with the plumbing, or you have to stop and take the sick cat to the veterinarian, or the school calls and tells you Johnny fell and skinned his knee. You might say that the domestic part of running a home business keeps us humble.

Break tasks down into 22-minute segments, as we discussed for office projects. If you have a large task that needs to be done, like cleaning out the pantry, a closet, or garage, don't let it overwhelm you. Once you are overwhelmed, you will tend to put it off and it will never be completed. Instead, set a timer for 22 minutes and get as much done in that time as possible. Then, next time you have an additional 22 minutes, continue doing some more, and so on. If you use the 22-minute rule, you will actually get a task done faster than if you wait until you "find" hours of extra time to do it later.

Does the whole family help with domestic duties? Do you need help? Do you know how to train your children to be better organized? Is there a way to save time on grocery day? How do you develop a home filing system? What are faster ways of cleaning out the garage? These are a few of the questions you will find answers to in this chapter.

SIMPLIFY PROCEDURES AT HOME

Save time and effort by making things easier. Each time you begin a task, stop and think about any shortcuts or faster ways that project could be handled. Once you are tuned in to trying to figure out better methods, you will create and streamline many techniques. If you are doing something now in five steps, try to find a way to do it in three steps. Use waiting time when browning meat or boiling water to begin wiping down countertops or to clean up a spill. Wipe counters in a two-fisted manner. In one hand you might have a sponge scraper for tough, dried-on food and in the other a rag to clean it up after it is loosened.

Washing Dishes.   While you are waiting for food to cook, begin soaking pots and pans. Rather than carrying a large pot or skillet to the sink to soak, bring the water to the dirty pot by using the sprayer on your sink. If you don't have a sprayer, save yourself from carrying the heavy water-filled pan by carrying a pitcher of water to soak the pan. While you are washing dishes, have other dishes soaking in soapy water or in a place where your rinse water runs over them. Then, by the time you are ready to wash the remainder of the dishes, they will be easier to clean.

Loading the Dishwasher. If loading the dishwasher always hurts your back, load three or four items at one time to cut your back-bending time. To save time and effort, load the dishwasher from back to front. This way you don't have to reach over items to place other items behind them. Load all the large plates in one area and all the small plates together in another when putting dishes away. This allows you to grab four or five plates at a time and they are already stacked and ready to be placed on the shelves. The same rule holds true for loading dirty cups and glasses. Place the cups in close proximity and the glasses next to other glasses. When unloading the dishwasher, carry the silverware holder over to the drawer and grab all the knives to put away at the same time, then all the forks, and so on.

Doing the Laundry. The biggest mistake made in performing laundry chores is not having the supplies (detergent, softener, or bleach) in the immediate area of the washer and dryer. Even if you have to install a shelf, so that you have everything handy, do it! Storing the supplies down the hall and having to put them away afterward just doesn't work. Remember, anything that saves steps is also saving time. When you take clothes out of a dryer, hang them immediately, before wrinkles set in. Don't dry more than four shirts or four pants at a time. They come out ready to wear, and it will save ironing time. Have a rack with empty hangers handy to hang clothes. If you must iron, do it while listening to a cassette tape, talking to a friend, or watching a TV show. Doing something will make the job easier and the time go faster. The same thing is true of folding clothes. Listen or talk while folding and it won't be such a bothersome task.

Setting the Table. Too many people have to run to another part of the house to find the place mats or tablecloth when the table needs setting. Be sure your place mats, napkins, and other tableware are kept close to the dining room or kitchen table so they are easily accessible. There are many attach-a-shelf units available now that are wonderful for adding extra shelf space. Some are made just the size to hold place mats. Even if you don't have the room to keep all the napkins and tablecloths close by, at least keep the ones that are used daily.

Cooking Meals. Make a deal that whoever is home first starts the meal. Since you are the one with the home-based business, it will most likely be you. So, face up to it and at least start the meal before your spouse arrives. If you prepare the meal, then the other one gets cleanup duty after the meal. Take turns cooking and cleaning up. Even let the kids take a specific night each week to prepare a meal. Even if it is hot dogs, who cares? It teaches them to want to help, and having responsibilities gives them confidence and a value system.

Clearing the Table.   Take a lesson from the busboys in the restaurants and bus your home table. Take a large plastic rectangular container and scrape and stack all dishes from the table at once to save many trips back and forth from the table to the sink. They are also easier to wash or load into the

HOUSEWORK . . .
Shouldn't Something This Wonderful
Be Shared?

dishwasher when they are together. While you are still visiting over the table after a meal, put lids on serving dishes, place all silverware together, and use a rubber scraper to clean off the dirty plates.

When you are ready to put leftovers away, take the storage containers to the table instead of carrying the food out to the kitchen to dump into containers.

CLUTTER CONTROL FOR THE HOME

Don't suffer in silence by feeling like you have to do it all. Ask others for help. Many husbands don't help because they have never been asked. Remember, no one can read your mind. If you are upset about having to do it all, tell him! Talk about ways you might be able to solve the situation. One single lady I know says she hates to clean bathrooms and a friend of hers hates to clean kitchens. So, they have a working relationship: Once a week, the friend cleans her bathroom and she cleans the friend's kitchen. She says it is more fun to break up the monotony by cleaning for someone else once in a while. Families, can do chores together for the greatest satisfaction and enjoyment. Whether the family does housecleaning or yard work together, the job goes faster and is more fun. Are you sharing the household duties with each family member? There is no reason why Mom should have to do all the picking up or make all the beds. Make everyone responsible for their own room.

1. Start out by having a family meeting to talk about what needs to be done.
2. Have everyone make a list of what duties they are responsible for: dishes, garbage, cleaning the bird cage, etc.
3. When the lists are all completed, discuss them and compare to see who is getting by without helping as much as they might.
4. Even out the lists by assigning certain duties to each adult or child.

Ask each person what duties they would *like* to do. They won't mind as much if they are asked for input. Only *assign* jobs if you have to. And, then it is important to rotate jobs so no one gets bored. Don't have Mike always take out the trash and Judy always do the dishes. Trade off tasks to keep it more interesting. This is the best way to teach children a sense of responsibility, delegation, and how to make trades. If one child cannot follow through with his or her job one day, let him "make a deal" with another child to trade off duties. But, let that child be responsible for finding another person to get the job done. This allows children to be creative. Monitor their negotiations, of course, to be sure no one is being manipulated.

To be sure you and your spouse are sharing the load equally, here is a form to use. Indicate with a check mark who is now responsible for each area:

	Me	Him	Things We Share	Things Children Can Help With
Grocery Shopping	_____	_____	_____	_____
Cooking	_____	_____	_____	_____
Cleaning House	_____	_____	_____	_____
• trash duties	_____	_____	_____	_____
Washing Dishes	_____	_____	_____	_____
• drying	_____	_____	_____	_____
• unloading dishwasher	_____	_____	_____	_____
Laundry	_____	_____	_____	_____
Lawn Mowing	_____	_____	_____	_____
• trimming	_____	_____	_____	_____
• raking	_____	_____	_____	_____
• edging	_____	_____	_____	_____
• sweeping	_____	_____	_____	_____
House Maintenance	_____	_____	_____	_____
• repairs	_____	_____	_____	_____
Car Maintenance	_____	_____	_____	_____
• cleaning	_____	_____	_____	_____
• repairing	_____	_____	_____	_____
Children	_____	_____	_____	_____
• taxi service	_____	_____	_____	_____
• clothes shopping	_____	_____	_____	_____
• doctor/dentist appts.	_____	_____	_____	_____
• who stays home when they are sick	_____	_____	_____	_____
• other activities	_____	_____	_____	_____
Running Household Errands	_____	_____	_____	_____
• attending PTA	_____	_____	_____	_____
• stopping for bread/ milk	_____	_____	_____	_____
• cleaners	_____	_____	_____	_____
• bank	_____	_____	_____	_____

Pets

- trips to vet
- grooming
- buying pet food

Earning Income

Making Investments

Finances

- balancing checkbook
- paying bills
- budgeting
- income tax records

One couple, who rarely see each other because of their job careers, love to do things together. So, when they are both at home, rather than him doing something in one room and her doing something in a different room, they share their time together. If she is cooking, he cleans up the dishes. Or if he is in the mood to cook, she cleans up. When there is yard work to be done, they are both in the yard until it's finished. They visit and enjoy each other by making their time together "prime time."

Housework

Always dress for the job. If you are already dressed in a suit for an appointment, don't be surprised if you don't get much done around the house before you leave. You wouldn't consider showing up at a business appointment in jeans and a sweatshirt, so don't expect to get much housework done with a suit or high heels on. Before you start the housework, prioritize what needs to be done most. If you are having company that night and they will only be in the living room or the kitchen, don't worry about cleaning the bedroom. If there is time (or energy) left when you are through accomplishing the priorities, then go ahead and clean the bedroom.

Getting the family involved in housework. Designate a certain time each night before the children have to be in bed and turn on a timer for 10 minutes of pick up time. Everyone is to pick up their own items and put them in their places. No one objects to 10 short minutes and it saves one person from spending hours picking up the next day. A free-lance writer said she sets aside 15 minutes in her office as pick up time during the day. This helps her keep things where they belong. In a multilevel house, set things on the stairs, with each child's name taped to the wall by a stair. Whenever you find something during the day that needs to go in that child's room, stack it on the stair with his name. Train the children to always pick up whatever is by their name and take it to their room when they go upstairs.

Tip: Family members will become more involved if you don't pick at the way they perform a task. Let them do it their way. Nagging will make them resent helping. Accept their way and realize they are not you and will do things differently than you would.

Are you setting an example for your toddlers by putting your clothes away? Take notice of what example you are giving by making the beds, hanging up clothes, or picking up after yourself. If Mom and Dad's room and closet is neat and in order, children will want theirs tidy too. Mimicking adults is the way children learn.

When doing housework, have all cleaning supplies handy. A carpenter's apron is an excellent way of carrying extra little rags, small tools, and supplies from room to room. Or, carry a small bucket with supplies. Normal cleaning supplies like ammonia, toilet bowl cleaner, bathtub brush, glass cleaner, and sponges should all be stored in several locations. If you have two bathrooms, have all the cleaning supplies available in each bathroom. This saves you running back and forth "sharing" supplies. If you have a two-story house, never allow yourself to run up and down stairs. Clean one floor thoroughly, then the other.

Establish a self-payment plan.   When you do complete a lengthy or difficult project, decide how you will reward yourself. You might decide the payment, once the task is done, will be to read a favorite magazine or allow yourself 20 minutes to call a friend on the phone. If you love to shop, glance through a new catalog. While you are actually doing the task, be thinking and planning what your self-payment will be. Make it something you really love to do so it serves as incentive to get the dreaded task done.

How Children Can Help

Post bathroom rules. List whatever things are important to you in keeping the bathroom clean. Tape a large piece of paper to the back of the bathroom door that says something like this:

Before you leave please check to be sure:

1. Cap is on the toothpaste
2. Toilet is flushed
3. Towels are hung
4. Clothes are removed
5. Soap is replaced
6. Sink is clean

Also, make it easy for children to keep their rooms clean. They won't mind picking up if you make it a game. (Offer a prize to whoever can pick up things the fastest.) Let children choose the color of their bedroom because they will have more desire to keep it nice if it is painted *their* favorite color. A child can usually make a bed with a quilt or coverlet, rather than a bedspread. Put shelf units as well as closet rods low enough so they can reach them.

When cleaning a room, let children help clean one part while you clean another. Then, you can talk while you are doing it. Guide them in how it should be done, when they seem open to learning. Make it fun for them to help.

MAKE GROCERY DAY EASIER

Have you ever wished there was a faster method for getting grocery day out of the way? One day I realized what we all go through to have full cupboards. We handle each item too many times. First, we pick it out and put it in the crooked grocery cart. (They never go straight, do they?) Then each item is taken back out of the cart to be checked. Now a grocery bagger handles it again to put it in sacks. Then, into the trunk of the car only to be handled once or twice again when we unpack it and put it on the shelf. YUK—that is really a ritual that we can all do without. *There must be a better way,* I thought to myself. So, out of desperation from spending almost three hours in the grocery store every two weeks, I developed a faster, easier method of getting groceries. If you are like me, you would rather be doing *anything* else besides buying groceries. Before we discuss the nuts and bolts of this simple procedure, let's start with the basics:

1. Choose one store for *all* your shopping. It is a proven fact that you do not save any money by running to every store in town for their specials. When you figure your time and gas, it will make you a believer.
2. Shop when stores are least crowded. If you must shop on weekends, shop off-pay weekends. Not on the first or fifteenth of the month, though. Other bad times are between 5:00 and 7:00 P.M. or Saturday and Sunday afternoons.
3. Never shop on an empty stomach or you will pick up all the junk and snack foods without realizing it.
4. Shop only every two weeks so you can stick to a budget. The secret is to never run out of anything! You will never again experience the tension of having to run to the store in the middle of preparing dinner to get that "missing" ingredient.

Make a Permanent List

To do this properly, you need to have a floor layout map of the store.

Sometimes the supermarkets have them already made up and just for the asking. If they do not, spend ten minutes and make your own by jotting down the aisle number and categories of each aisle. When you get home, begin making your "main" shopping list by writing down the items you normally buy in each aisle while glancing at the store map. Leave some blanks in each aisle to fill in later with new or seldom-bought items. If you do not have a baby or pet, do not put these aisles on your list at all. Now all you do is type or print your main list and make copies.

Always keep a list posted on your refrigerator so the entire family can participate by circling an item when they notice it is half gone.

Plan Meals

Before you leave for the store, plan how many breakfasts, lunches, and dinners you estimate you will be preparing over the next two-week period after allowing for the number of times you eat out. You may want to plan to have various entrees such as fish, pork, chicken, and beef during these two weeks. For variety, I like to plan some Italian, Mexican, and German dishes to be sure I have different choices. Leave one or two meals "unplanned" so you will have a little flexibility and use some creativity for a new dish. Plan not only the meat dish, but the vegetable, salad, and bread you intend to serve with each meal. If you flip through your recipe box, you will come up with great ideas.

On the back of your grocery list write down all the menus you have decided to cook this grocery period. Now pull each recipe and check to be certain you have all the necessary ingredients on hand. If not, add them to your list. *Do not* refile the recipe. Instead, stand it up on end in the back of your recipe box. This way when you are ready to prepare the dish, you don't have to search for it again.

Coupon Clipping. If you are a coupon clipper, discipline yourself to clip coupons only for what you actually buy. Otherwise, money is wasted by trying a new item just because there is a coupon. After the entire grocery list is complete, check through your coupons while comparing them to your list. *Caution:* Do not take a folder or shoe box of coupons to the store and waste time going through them on the premises. (You'll be there so long we will have to feed you intravenously.) If you check through your list in advance, then you can have with you only the coupons you intend to use. Note on your list whether you have a coupon for Maxwell House or Hill's Brothers coffee by putting the initials next to the item. Then you don't have to shuffle through the entire pile of coupons. If you don't particularly care whether you buy blueberry muffin mix by Betty Crocker or Duncan Hines, but you have a coupon for Betty Crocker, then mark B.C. next to it on the grocery list.

This streamlined method will cut grocery shopping time to about 30 minutes. That's a whole lot better than three hours, right? Now you have time to concentrate on doing some things you like to do. Happy shopping!

MENU PLANNING AND FOOD STORAGE

When you have an office at home, you still have to stop and prepare meals for yourself or the family. Here are some tips to save you time, trouble, and money. Whether you are getting ready for a dinner party or preparing normal meals, planning is the secret and needs to be done ahead. If you have to cook anyway, then prepare a double recipe. It isn't any more trouble and spells *L-E-F-T-O-V-E-R-S*. Cook large roasts, double casseroles, soups, and stews. On the mornings you know you will not have time to cook, pull leftovers out of the freezer and *voila!* It will look as if you slaved away in the kitchen the entire day. You may even discover that you enjoy cooking more when you don't have to be concerned about cooking every single night.

If you buy beef, consider purchasing it in large quantities when it is on sale. Or, go to a meat market where you can order a quarter or a half beef. Purchase large cuts of meat at the grocer and have them cut it in half to serve two meals.

Purchase extra supplies when they are on sale. This is especially true of breads because they freeze so well. All you need to do is double wrap them in plastic bread wrappers and they freeze beautifully. Rolls, vegetables, desserts, almost anything freezes well except for whipping cream or egg-white type frostings.

When you freeze, wrap meal-size portions. For instance, if you live alone, freeze separate pieces of lasagna or one beef patty to a package. Be sure the contents, date, and weight are marked on the outside. If you have a family of four then package four chicken breasts, four veal cutlets, etc. On the outside of the freezer keep a list of exactly what meats and casseroles are contained inside.

Each time you remove a package from the freezer, also cross it off the freezer list posted on the front or top of the freezer itself. On grocery day you will be able to see quickly what you already have and what you need.

Freeze foods quickly. Do not overload your freezer with unfrozen food. Too much will slow down the freezing rate and the food could spoil or lose quality. Arrange packages you want frozen in a single layer, allowing a little air space between and around them. After they are frozen solid, they may be stacked together to save space. Keep it cold. Maintain a freezer temperature of zero degrees, or lower, for a maximum storage life.

Be sure to use everything in the freezer within recommended storage time. Label all packages. Use the oldest packages first by rotating the ones on the

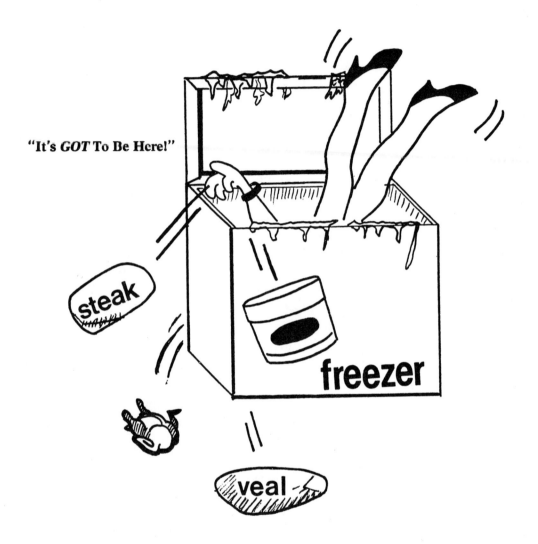

"It's *GOT* To Be Here!"

bottom before adding more packages on top. Avoid refreezing completely
thawed foods. When freezing any liquid or semi-liquid foods, allow for ex-
pansion during freezing to prevent leaking or bulging containers. About one
inch of headspace is sufficient for a quart-size container.

To avoid being without your casserole dishes due to freezer storage, line
the dish with foil, fill, and freeze. When the casserole is frozen, lift foil and
contents from the dish, wrap, and store it. When you're ready to use it, replace
the food in casserole dish for heating. Use ice cube trays for freezing small
amounts of broth, soup, or pureed baby food. When frozen, place the cubes in
plastic bags for storage.

Tip: If you choose to freeze in foil, do not freeze casseroles containing
tomato paste or sauce. The acid will eat through foil.

White freezer paper is the best material for packaging. Since the shiny side
is coated, the food is protected from freezer burn.

ESTABLISH A HOME FILING SYSTEM

It is imperative that you keep your home filing system separate from your office files. Set up your personal filing system alphabetically. Make a few general files, even if they are very thick, rather than having tons of individual files. When you do make a new file, be sure you have at least four items in it. If these general files get too thick, then begin making others with specific headings. Custom design your own file headings and put things under headings the way they come to your mind (so you'll be able to find papers when you need them). Here are some typical file headings and what would go into each one:

Car—service records, copy of registration, maintenance information, insurance policy

Checking Account—monthly statements, cancelled checks (sort yearly)

Children's Files (one for each child)—Little League schedules, calendar of events, class schedules, artwork, Boy Scouts, etc.

Clubs—organizations you belong to and their monthly newsletters

Dogs/Cats—shots, health records, licenses

House—garage sales, household hints, piano tuners, maid services

** Important Papers—Financial Picture (*see* page 125), *copies* of wills, IRAs, profit sharing, birth/marriage certificates. (Keep *originals* of wills and IRAs with a lawyer.) Include a large envelope for income tax receipts. *In case of an emergency:* each family member's Social Security number, driver's license number, car plates, year, model, and vehicle number should be listed

Insurance—pending claims, past claims, mortgage insurance, life policies

Interior Decorating—paint samples, how-to pamphlets, magazine pictures

Medical—health history, immunizations, broken bones, accidents, etc.

Miscellaneous—newspaper/magazine articles, diets

Outdoor—landscape sketch of front/backyard with all plant names, gardening tips, calendar of fertilizing/weed control, sprinkler system

Résumés—recommendation letters, personal reference letters, etc.

Major Purchases—major appliances, furs, antiques, instruction manuals, warranties, and guarantees

Minor Purchases—receipts for small appliances and any items under $100, warranty information

Vacation/Entertainment—brochures, newspaper clippings on places to go/things to do. Information on what you liked and didn't like about each trip. List items you need to remember next time.

None of us likes to think about a crisis happening, but we must be prepared in case of emergency. If an accident or death ever strikes a member of your family, would you know where to find important papers with critical information on insurance policies, savings accounts, relatives' contact phone numbers, investments, and so on? Make a colored (red works well) file and mark it "Important Papers." Your loved ones should all be aware of where this file is kept. Be sure it is always up to date. Mark on your calendar to update the information at least twice a year with policy numbers, contact phone numbers, and other pertinent information. This financial picture of your life should be easily accessible. This will be the most important paper you have in your home. (*See* sample on page 125.)

Do you have a will? A will is an absolute necessity unless you don't care what happens to your money and your possessions after you are gone. But even the most thorough will in the world won't do you any good if your heirs cannot locate it. Ask friends or other family members to recommend a good estate lawyer. Once you have had a will drawn up, tell your executor where to find it. Attach a copy of the "Important Papers" that tells where your records, property, and assets are located.

From time to time, be sure to go over the list to make appropriate changes. Do not scratch out or erase anything in your will or it is invalidated. To change a will, a new one must be executed or an amendment produced for the existing one. Where do you keep an original will? In your lawyer's safe is the best place. *Do not* keep it in your own safety deposit box. When you die, your bank will place a freeze on the contents.

Make an additional sheet to keep track of family information for contacting relatives in case of emergency. A sample to follow is shown on page 126.

Household Inventory

Few people have an accurate inventory of household belongings in case of a fire or robbery. We all think fires or burglaries can't "happen to me." Unfortunately, it *can* happen to you. Just being a victim of a robbery or a fire is bad enough, but not knowing precisely what was stolen or burned or its value only worsens the situation.

This is why it is so vital that you keep a Household Inventory. (*See* sample on page 127.) List all your household items for every room in the house. Chances are your home office includes some valuable electronics as well as the televisions, furniture, and other items that would need to be replaced. I've included a sample page for you to copy, or you can ask your homeowners' insurance company for a booklet to use. Make a separate sheet for every room in the house. Fill in the name of each room at the top of the page. Under "item" list every piece of furniture and other belongings. Be sure to write a good description and include any identifying marks such as scratches, dents, or chips. If there are any serial numbers or identification numbers, these are the best descriptions of all. What is the "value" of each item?

THIS WILL BE THE MOST IMPORTANT PAPER YOU HAVE IN YOUR HOME. Keep it updated yearly. If you have any family emergency, this information will allow fast contact with insurance policies, investments, savings accounts, etc. This financial picture of your life should be easily accessible. Flag it by using a *red* tab in your Important Papers file.

FINANCIAL PICTURE FOR JOHN & MARY DOE

As of _____ _____
   (month)   (year)

POLICY/ACCOUNT	COMPANY	ADDRESS	PHONE	NAME ON POLICY	AMOUNT	CONTACT PERSON/COMPANY	ACCOUNT/POLICY NO.
CHECKING ACCT.	:	Carrollton, TX	:	John	$:	:	# :
SAVINGS ACCT.	:	:	:	Mary	:	:	:
SAVINGS ACCT.	:	:	:	John	:	:	:
IRA	:	:	:	John	:	:	:
LIFE INSUR.	:	:	:	John	:	:	:
LIFE INSUR.	:	:	:	Mary	:	:	:
LIFE INSUR.	:	:	:	John	:	:	
HEALTH INSUR.	:	:	:	:	:	:	
HOMEOWNERS INSUR.	:	:	:	House	:	:	:
AUTOMOBILE	:	:	:	Olds Cutlass	:	:	:

GENERAL INFORMATION

House Mortgage is with _____   Mortgage Company   :
111 Speedway
Dallas, TX

In Case of Emergency Notify:

(*List full names*)	Relationship	Address & Phone
Martha Ann Jones	daughter	2424 Stevens Street Milwaukee, Wisconsin 79069 (203) 456-7890
Jack R. Smith	son	1000 Bay Street Mesquite, Texas 79030 (214) 234-5667

Mary's family:

Carl & Barbara Downs	parents	_____
Joan Lewis	sister	_____
Steve Harris	brother	_____

John's family:

Sam & Suzie Doe	parents	_____
Kevin Doe	brother	_____

(Be sure to list parents' first names. That will make them easier to contact.)

ROOM _____

ITEM	DESCRIPTION AND/OR IDENTIFYING MARKS	$ VALUE

This household inventory will be extremely helpful to police officers and insurance agents if something happens. It also gives you a clear record of what your household goods amount to so you can be sure you have proper insurance coverage. You will be surprised at how much you have accumulated in material possessions over the years. Keep these household inventory sheets in your "Important Papers" file and copies in your safe-deposit box.

8
When You Are Ready—Hire Help!

BEING SELF-SUFFICIENT is one thing, but don't get ridiculous. When you are handling your own sales, marketing, computer entry, correspondence, errands, accounting, and documentation as most home-business owners do, you need to stop periodically and ask yourself if you are spending time doing what you do best. Is there something else you could be doing that would be more profitable? Would it be beneficial to have help to do the work or run errands from time to time? For example, if you are spending hours running to the copy machine when you could be writing a newsletter to attract more customers, you need to realize you are wasting your talent and money.

How do you stay in control of a growing business so it doesn't control you? The task that owners fear most is that of hiring. The thought of having someone in your home will always conjure up worries of being burglarized or cheated, or feelings that your privacy has been invaded. But, don't forget, in any office, even in large businesses, the employer's fears are the same. In the large office atmosphere, another worker can just as easily steal from your office or go through your desk invading your privacy.

Don't let fear prevent you from achieving the success you are working toward. Hire the best people you can get and pay them a competitive salary. Then, don't worry—just get on with the business at hand. You can never have a profitable business until you expand and hire others to assist you. Otherwise, you are limiting your own potential.

Because home-based business owners tend to be self-sufficient, it is easy to spread ourselves too thin by trying to do everything. To know when you are ready to hire additional help, you must rely on your intuition and your work load. The number one rule is, don't be "penny-wise and pound-foolish"! One marketing consultant said if she had to start her business all over again, she would "hire help sooner." When you are used to doing it all, it is difficult to realize when it is time to relinquish and delegate duties to others. For example, if you find yourself rushing all over town on business errands rather than spending time selling yourself or marketing, you are being penny-wise and pound-foolish. This "penny-wise, pound-foolish" syndrome seems to be a common denominator among home-based business owners everywhere. When you have developed your business, be smarter than most and know when the syndrome strikes.

To determine whether to hire a part-time or full-time person, keep a log for two weeks of all the tasks, errands, computer entry, collating, copying, and phone calls that you take care of now. After this period of time, look over the list and mark each task as to whether it could have been handled by someone else. Jot down alongside each item how long the task required. Add up the total hours and divide by two to get the average number of hours you will need help over a week's time. If the hours needed are under 20, hire part-time help. If the total comes closer to 40 hours, it's clear that you could keep a full-time person busy.

Be aware that paying a new employee isn't the only cost you'll encounter. There will be taxes and fringe benefits that can run as high as 40 percent above salary costs. If you're not sure how much help you need, try some part-time or temporary help until you decide whether you need a full-time person. You can find people who are looking for part-time work by advertising in your local newspaper or on the church bulletin board. Many former secretaries would reply to an ad that says, "Work 10:00 to 2:00 while the kids are in school." If you live in an apartment, post a "Help Wanted" notice in the laundry facility. Distributive Education students from your local high schools are always looking for part-time work after school or on weekends. Also, call your local rehabilitation institute. They offer excellent skills from people who have physical disabilities. Many times the institute has job banks that match the requirements of the position with their patients' qualifications. You can arrange to either drop off work and pick it up or have a person come into your home.

If what you really need is an office manager, then hire the right person for the job. Remember, even if you have to spend more for a good worker, it may be worth it if he or she saves you time, markets you well, and promotes business. A good office manager-type will probably cost you $300 to $400 a week (in most areas of the country).

If you need to hire a salesperson, be sure you look for a person who is good over the phone and in person. Many times you can find a salesperson who will work on a commission-only basis rather than salary. This is an excellent arrangement because you aren't paying for their services unless they sell your product or services. You will never go "in the hole" paying commission.

Tip: Do not hire friends or relatives. If a friend doesn't work out as an employee, then you may lose both the employee and the relationship.

INTERVIEWING IDEAS

In order to compare apples to apples, and to avoid discriminatory lawsuits, always have applicants fill out the same application form. A pad of applications can be purchased at any office supply store. This also makes the job of screening easier as you view "like" forms. Planning for the job interview is critical to finding the right person. To help you prepare, here are some specifics you'll want to list:

• The job description in detail
• Your objectives and goals for your business
• Various tasks they will be expected to perform
• Skills needed to do the work

- Working conditions
- Education needed
- Physical requirements

One element of successful interviewing is to let the applicants talk 70 percent of the time. This is how you learn about their personalities, their goals, their personal lives, and so on. Since law doesn't allow you to ask any discriminatory questions, you have to hope they will offer information about themselves that you need to know. Being "all ears" is the *only* way to investigate their attitudes, work background, and whether they will be compatible with your specifications.

$ $ $ Success Brief $ $ $

After only 18 months of having her home business as sales director for **Mary Kay Cosmetics**, Suzi Unumb now makes four to five times more money than she did as a marketing director of a property management company. She currently manages 97 people and attributes her own success to having a great trainer and role model. "Hiring the right people for your team is important. I look for people with self-confidence, goals, and a vision."

$ $ $

Listening is the key to finding out if the two of you are a good match. Listen for positives and negatives to give you clues of how they view themselves and their degree of self-confidence. An employee's level of optimism is the best predictor of his or her success.

Before starting the interview process, visit with the applicants to warm them up. Never sit across a desk from them. The interview will be much more personal and comfortable if you sit next to them, indicating you are putting yourself on the same level with them.

Whether you are looking for a full- or part-time person, always ask open-ended questions rather than the type that can be answered yes or no. Here are some questions that will tell you a great deal about an applicant:

1. *What attracted you to answer the ad?* If the answer is, "the hours," or, "the money," this may not be the best person for you. But, if he comments about wanting to grow in your type of business or says that the job sounds challenging, you've got a prospect.
2. *What are your hobbies?* Someone who says, "watching TV," probably doesn't have much initiative or ambition. On the other hand, a person who enjoys taking educational classes or is active in sports, shows a desire to learn and to stay physically and mentally fit.
3. *What do you do for fun?* This one can really open up a conversation. Listen carefully for things you do or do not want to hear.
4. *What did you like best about your last position? Least?* If the answer is, "I liked the breaks and lunchtime best," you can see a lack of dedication and what kind of worker this person will be.

5. *Why does this position interest you?* If the only comment is, "Because it's close to home," look further.
6. *Describe your ideal job.* Listen to see if the description given is anything like the job you're interviewing for.
7. *Can you work various hours or overtime, if needed?* Since you are not allowed to ask specific questions about children, this answer will usually mention if the employee would need notice of working late in order to find a baby-sitter, etc.
8. *On a scale of 1 to 10, how positive a person are you? Explain why?* This is where you listen for the level of optimism versus pessimism.
9. *Tell me about your goals. . . . Where do you see yourself five years from now?* If the answer is, "I want to have my own business," the applicant is showing his ambitious side. This person would be a great employee because he wants to grow.
10. *Do you prefer being trained by someone or learning on your own?* Anyone who prefers learning on his own rather than being shown every little thing has real moxie.
11. *What have you enjoyed most in your career as a __(title)__?*
12. *What would your three strengths in this position be? Your three weaknesses?*

Tip: Always ask for and check out references before hiring. Many "wrong" employees can be avoided by checking references beforehand.

Don't ever let someone else hire for you. You must meet and talk with someone yourself to know whether your personalities mesh. Even when your home business grows to many employees and departments, one important thing to remember is to always let the supervisor or department head do his own hiring. Nothing is worse than a new employee being hired by personnel and being "placed" in a department. This method of hiring seldom works and is usually the cause of personality conflicts. Be sure to give yourself and the new employee a 90-day probationary (trial) period. This is fair to both of you in case it doesn't work out.

How to Give an Orientation

You took the time to hire the right people, now give them a proper orientation about you and your business. A good orientation makes people feel they belong. Give them a tour of your home office, showing them everything from where the supplies are kept to where the water glasses and the bathroom are located. Use a checklist to be sure you cover all topics:

• **Introduction**—If you already have people working for you, take time to introduce them.

- **Guided Tour**—Show them around: copy machine, mail area, refrigerator, etc.
- **Explain Philosophy**—Tell them your business philosophy and history.
- **Salary program/benefits**—Give them complete information on their salary, paydays, benefits, and hours they are to work.
- **Training**—Give them a clear, well-defined job description or reference guide.
- **Rules**—Explain any specific rules and regulations they are to follow.
- **Advancement**—Explain the possibilities for promotions or raises.

The more they understand about you and what your expectations are, the better job they will be able to do for you.

CREATING A JOB DESCRIPTION

Whether you hire a secretary, bookkeeper, computer operator, or a clerk, write out a Job Description Reference Guide for them to use. When you train new employees, you normally spend a lot of time showing and explaining *how* and *what* is expected of them. Each new person has to interrupt you many times a day to ask about work procedures. To cut training time by at least 50 percent, prepare a reference guide they can refer to when they have questions. It saves you and the new person a lot of frustration. Did you know the main reason new employees fail is *not knowing what is expected* of them? Studies show 70 percent of all workers were not sure what was expected of them on any given workday.

Tell them what your likes and dislikes are. For instance, if you hate employees wasting time on personal phone calls, tell them. If you like a worker who doesn't watch the clock and charge out the door at 5:00, tell them. They can't read your mind.

Each employee should keep his or her own Job Reference Guide on their desk for easy access. Use this Table of Contents as an example, but custom design your own. It should contain procedures and guidelines that are important to you and your business. Here are ideas as to what your Job Reference Guide might include:

Table of Contents

Opening and Closing the Office 1
Telephone Techniques 2
Accounts Receivable/Payable 3
Responsibilities and Procedures 5
Letter Formats 8
Word Processing How-to's 10
Copy Machine Duties 12

When you begin training your new person, be sure you give out information in phases. Dumping too much information at one time on a new person makes it impossible to absorb.

**Oversaturation Causes
Brain Damage**

Here are some ways to develop your new employees and help them do their best work:

- Tell them regularly what you want and how you want it done.
- Show them specific methods of sorting mail, letter formats you prefer, telephone techniques, what time of day to go the the post office box, etc.
- Give them positive and negative feedback on a regular basis.
- Keep them informed of matters that concern their jobs or schedules.
- Reward them with appreciation.
- Allow them to create and do their job. This supports self-worth and self-esteem.

DEVELOP PROBLEM-SOLVING SKILLS

As your business grows, so will the challenges you face. When you can solve problems more effectively, you can get ahead faster. Most leaders and high-level executives make it to the top because of their exceptional problem-solving skills. You do not have to be born with this ability. Anyone can develop and refine it. The following exercise will give you some special insights to solving problems:

Yes   No

- Are you willing to ask for help without hesitation when a problem arises?   _____

- Do you view work problems as a positive step to better opportunities?   _____

- Do you avoid doing too much research or study to obtain information needed to complete a project?   _____

- Do you make a steady effort to upgrade your ability to solve problems?   _____

- Do you have reliable sources/experts to call on for help when trying to solve problems?   _____

- Do you get all the information needed before deciding on a solution?   _____

Total *Yes* answers _____

If you score 6 or more *Yes* answers, congrats! You are doing an excellent job as a problem solver.

If you score 4 or 5, you are an average problem solver.

If you score 3 or less, you need to work harder. The ideas above will give you assistance.

When you are independent and confident, asking for help is very hard to do. One method of getting over the I-can-do-it-alone syndrome is to think about the consequences. If you are not willing to admit that you need a little advice on solving a problem or some suggestions and input, then you are going to waste a lot of time. Drawing on other people and their knowledge helps you learn faster. None of us knows it all. Sometimes you have to ask for assistance. Do it, then go on about your business. It is a skill that becomes easier as you practice it.

**The Cart Goes a Lot Faster If
We're All Pulling It
in the Same Direction**

USE TEAMWORK PRINCIPLES

Working together as a team, with one common goal, is critically important to your professional success. Standing over the workers' shoulders demanding and commanding is no longer an acceptable style of supervision. As an employer, you will want to work together with your employee(s) to build bridges and achieve your objectives. When people work together, it is called "team management." Sometimes it takes getting in the trenches with your employees. Show me a supervisor or manager who is respected by his workers, and I'll show you a person who digs in *with* his employees to get the work done rather than ordering them to do it. This is the way to get the best results. Allow people to participate in the management of your company, not just do the work. This creates more job satisfaction and loyalty. You will have less turnover and more productivity. To make the teamwork principle happen, you must:

- Help solve problems and get people involved
- Display a positive attitude with employees
- Invite open communication
- Be consistent in your decisions in order to gain their respect
- Listen to their ideas and offer feedback
- Share business objectives and work together to achieve them

There are four main bones in every organization:
THE WISHBONES
wishing somebody would do
something about it
THE JAWBONES
doing all the talking
but nothing else
THE KNUCKLEBONES
that knock everything
THE BACKBONE
that carries the load and
does the work

The secret is finding ways to make all your employees "backbones." Employees need to feel they are an important part of your business. If you meet their needs, and work side by side with them you have teamwork. How do you motivate people to be backbones? Even though this survey was taken among employees of hundreds of our largest corporations, workers agree that these things are what motivates them most:

Financial Security—Workers need to be paid fairly for their time and effort to feel a sense of reward.
Emotional Support—Employees need to feel their job and input contributes to a worthwhile goal.
Recognition—Employees have to know that good work will be appreciated and acknowledged.
Self-Expression—Employees need to be able to communicate suggestions, ideas, and opinions without being afraid of the consequences.
Respect—Employees need to be treated like people, not numbers.

The employees who make the best workers are proud of what they do. How can you help instill this pride? One way is by giving your employees personalized business cards (name and title). You can have the cards printed for about $25. The benefit is two-fold: It encourages pride in their work and it gives your business extra marketing as the cards are handed out. And, what a great way to welcome a new employee as a part of your team. There are many other ways to build employees to peak performing standards.

BUILDING EMPLOYEE MORALE

Great employee morale doesn't just happen. You have to work at it on a regular basis. **Make a plan** of specific methods you can use to improve morale. To build loyalty, you must build people!

What are the benefits of boosting morale? If employees are happy and feel they are an asset, there is no limit to how high your business can soar. Employee satisfaction will result in less absenteeism and turnover, more productivity and profit. Here are some ideas that have proved successful in morale building for any size business:

1. Acknowledge an employee's extra contribution by:

* giving him a pat on the back
* telling him one-on-one
* writing a thank-you note

2. Distribute trade magazines, publications, and "good letters" weekly that deal with company morale. When you spot a positive article or story in a magazine that would raise morale, make copies and distribute them to all employees.

Tip: Distributing articles also helps train a person to know what you like without constantly expressing yourself verbally. If you think something is important enough to copy it and pass it on to your employees, they will sense that you approve of the article and will take it to heart. A great opportunity for additional extra training!

Good letters: Make it a policy that anytime you receive a complimentary letter from a client, the letter is to be routed and posted. This tells employees that you are proud of their work.

3. Hold open general meetings —Whether you have 1 or 100 employees, have periodic open meetings. Ask for ideas and input. You will be surprised how creative they can be. They will also help you solve problems, if you let them.

4. Alternate job and task responsibilities to increase knowledge of your business, boost interest, and prevent boredom. Employees learn to better understand the "team" effort when they switch positions for a while. (Use the Job Description Reference Guide referred to earlier in this chapter to make alternating jobs easy.)

5. Gain input from staff on projects, ideas, suggestions. Ask them—they will show you various perspectives you may not see.

6. Learn to listen to their point of view without being critical. Listening lets them know their opinions count. Peter Drucker, management expert, says, "Don't be critical without listening to their point of view. The most frustrating thing in the world is NOT being heard."

7. Distribute attitude surveys at least every six months to get a handle on their feelings about job duties, morale level, and supervisory satisfaction. As your business grows you will wonder how employees feel about your company, about you as a boss, and about their responsibilities. Attitude surveys are your best resource—use them to your benefit. Many attitude surveys are available in library books.

8. Set an example —To gain their respect.

- Project a "good attitude" to employees at all times.
- Recognize them—call them by name. This personal touch shows that you care and makes them feel important.
- Don't walk in late or leave early.
- Don't ask anyone to do anything you wouldn't do yourself.
- Pitch in and work with them.

9. Provide a suggestion box —When you employ enough people, always have an anonymous suggestion box available. Many people who won't tell you in person *will* write down their feelings or opinions.

10. Encourage promotion —Give employees the opportunity to fill vacancies or new positions of *their* choice. Allow them to apply along with other outside applicants.

11. Provide training on new procedures and equipment to raise employees' knowledge level and their confidence. Show and teach people how to do things properly. It will save you time and money in the long run.

12. Encourage responsibility by allowing people to perform tasks with the least possible supervision.

13. Acknowledge employees' birthdays to stimulate stronger relationships. Celebrate business anniversaries with them.

14. Give performance feedback regularly through:

- verbal discussions on a regular basis
- written performance evaluations every six months

15. Give $$ rewards:

- year-end bonus
- special bonus for extraordinary work performance
- salary advancement based on performance evaluation

WRITING AND CONDUCTING PERFORMANCE EVALUATIONS

Giving **regular** performance feedback makes a difference in how your employee feels about his own work and about the company. He will think he is being ignored if you are not evaluating his performance either verbally or in writing.

Verbal evaluations should be done at least every three months. Sit down with the person and talk about daily functions and feelings. Most supervisors put off giving performance evaluations because (a) they dislike doing them, or (b) they don't feel the need to give input to employees.

Any particular incidents or situations you want to be sure to talk about in length can be kept in the employee's file in your desk. Whenever something occurs to you for discussion, thanks, or streamlining, jot it down in that person's folder so you won't forget it. This way when you sit down with him, you are prepared.

An evaluation might include grading in areas of initiative, promptness, or meeting deadlines. Here is a simple, easy-to-follow format to use in preparing for a verbal evaluation:

	WHAT BUGS ME	WHAT I LIKE THAT THEY DO	WHAT I WOULD LIKE TO SEE IMPROVED
Telephone Skills			
Quality of Work			
Handling People			
Paperwork Methods			
Efficiency			
Attitude			
Communication Skills			

Written evaluations should be done at least every six months. One idea that works well for many companies is to have the employees write up their own evaluations. Then, discuss it together!

The mistake most supervisors make is not reviewing the evaluation with the employee. Never just hand them their evaluation and walk off. It voids the purpose of completing one. Discussion shows you care to take the time and you both are able to grow through the process. When you are ready to research an evaluation format that would work best for you, there are hundreds of samples in library books.

Here is one guide to performance appraisal that proves they don't always have to be serious:

GUIDE TO PERFORMANCE APPRAISAL

(read across)

PERFORMANCE	FAR EXCEEDS JOB REQUIREMENTS	EXCEEDS JOB REQUIREMENTS	MEETS JOB REQUIREMENTS	NEEDS SOME IMPROVEMENT
QUALITY	Leaps tall buildings with a single bound	Must take running start to leap over tall buildings	Can leap over short buildings only	Crashes into buildings when attempting to leap over them
TIMELINESS	Is faster than a speeding bullet	Is as fast as a speeding bullet	Not quite as fast as a speeding bullet	Would you believe a slow bullet?
INITIATIVE	Is stronger than a locomotive	Is stronger than a bull elephant	Is stronger than a bull	Shoots the bull
ADAPTABILITY	Walks on water consistently	Walks on water in emergencies	Washes with water	Drinks water
COMMUNICATION	Talks with God	Talks with the angels	Talks to himself	Argues with himself

POSTSCRIPT

The moral of this book is that with good self-managment skills, a little creativity, a sense of humor, and faith in God, you will succeed in your home-business endeavor.

Believe, and you CAN do it!

REFERENCES AND RESOURCES

Listed are many books for your further reading. The books I have consulted while writing this book are marked with an asterisk.

Bliss, Edwin. *Getting Things Done.* 13th printing. New York: Bantam Books, 1985.

Brabec, Barbara. *Homemade Money: The Definitive Guide to Success in a Home Business.* 3rd. ed. Crozet, Va.: Betterway Publications, 1989.

Charlesworth, Edward A., and Ronald G. Nathan. *Stress Management: A Comprehensive Guide to Wellness.* New York: Ballantine Books, 1985.

Dean, Jan. *Money-Saving Tips for the Small Business Owner.* 2nd ed. Fort Worth, Texas: Lagniappe Publications, 1989.

*Delany, George, and Sandra Delany. *The #1 Home Business Book.* Blue Ridge Summit, Pa.: TAB Books, Inc., 1981.

Eisenberg, Ronni, and Kate Kelly. *Organize Yourself!* New York: Macmillan Publishing Company, Inc., 1986.

Feldman, Beverly N. *Homebased Businesses.* Los Angeles: Till Press, 1983.

Frohbieter-Mueller, Jo. *Stay Home & Mind Your Own Business.* Crozet, Va.: Betterway Publications, 1987.

*Gober, Mary, and Bob Tannehill. *The Art of Giving Quality Service.* Tannehill-Gober Associates International, 1984.

Hicks, Tyler G. *How to Start Your Own Business on a Shoestring.* Rocklin, Calif.: Prima Publishing and Communication, 1987.

Hutchcraft, Ronald. *Peaceful Living in a Stressful World.* Nashville: Thomas Nelson Publishers, 1985.

Selye, Hans. *Stress Without Distress.* New York: New American Library, 1975.

*Walther, George R. *Phone Power.* New York: Berkley Publishing, 1987.

Welch, Mary Scott. *Networking.* New York: Warner Books, 1981.

Cassette Tapes

Easy Self-Management, $10. Sharon Carr, 1987. "Time" of Your Life, 2800 Prescott Drive, Carrollton, TX 75006

Stress and You, $10. Sharon Carr, 1987. "Time" of Your Life, 2800 Prescott Drive, Carrollton, TX 75006

Team Management, $10. Sharon Carr, 1989. "Time" of Your Life, 2800 Prescott Drive, Carrollton, TX 75006

TMJ Pain Control: A Self-Help Program (2 tapes & manual), $29.95. Sharon Carr and
   Terry Daugherty, D.D.S., 1989. TMJ & Stress Center, P.O. Box 811094, Dallas, TX
   75381

Win and Keep Customers, $10. Sharon Carr, 1989. "Time" of Your Life, 2800 Prescott
   Drive, Carrollton, TX 75006

The Small Business Administration publishes many booklets to help a business get
started or maintain an existing business. You can obtain these publications at a
nominal fee (most are $.50 up to $1.00). Write to the U.S. Small Business Administration, P.O. Box 15434, Fort Worth, TX 76119 to request a complete list of available
material. Here are some specific ones that are very helpful:

Financial Management

"ABC's of Borrowing"
"Basic Budgets for Profit Planning"
"Budgeting in a Small Business Firm"
"Pricing Your Products and Services Profitably"
"Recordkeeping in a Small Business"
"Sound Cash Management and Borrowing"

General Management and Planning

"The Business Plan for Homebased Business"
"Developing a Strategic Business Plan"
"Effective Business Communications"
"Going Into Business"
"Planning and Goal Setting for Small Business"
"Problems in Managing a Family-Owned Business"
"Should You Lease or Buy Equipment?"
"Small Business Decision Making"

Marketing

"Advertising Media Decisions"
"Creative Selling: The Competitive Edge"
"Marketing for Small Business: An Overview"
"Marketing Checklist for Small Retailers"
"Research Your Market"

Personnel Management

"Checklist for Developing a Training Program"
"Employees: How to Find and Pay Them"
"Managing Employee Benefits"